T0281924

SCORCHED EARTH

SCORCHED EARTH

Beyond the Digital Age
to a Post-Capitalist World

Jonathan Crary

VERSO
London • New York

First published by Verso 2022
© Jonathan Crary 2022

3 5 7 9 10 8 6 4 2

Verso
UK: 6 Meard Street, London W1F 0EG
US: 20 Jay Street, Suite 1010, Brooklyn, NY 11201
versobooks.com
Verso is the imprint of New Left Books

ISBN-13: 978-1-78478-444-7
ISBN-13: 978-1-78478-446-1 (US EBK)
ISBN-13: 978-1-78478-445-4 (UK EBK)

British Library Cataloguing in Publication Data
A catalogue record for this book is available from the British Library

Library of Congress Cataloging-in-Publication Data
A catalog record for this book is available from the Library of Congress

Typeset in Garamond by Biblichor Ltd, Edinburgh
Printed and bound by CPI Group (UK) Ltd, Croydon, CR0 4YY

No don't say doom

—Tom Verlaine

Acknowledgments

I'm grateful to Sebastian Budgen and his colleagues at Verso for their continued backing of my work. For support and input of many kinds, my thanks and appreciation go to Hal Foster, Ron Clark, Federico Campagna, Andreas Malm, the late Bernard Stiegler, Michael Hardt, Yves Citton, Étienne Jollet, Sarah Cook, Jonathan Reekie, Cosima Dannoritzer, Ana Rovati, Uta Barth, Canada Choate, Tim Melley, Ruth Patir, Tali Keren, Greg Saunier and Deerhoof, Jon Wozencroft, Fergus Daly and Katherine Waugh, Brooke Holloway, Emmelyn Rosen-Butterfield, Marc Gottlieb, Michael Witt, Alyson Ogasian, Xueli Wang, Amy Powell, Eli Keller, Amity Law, Matt Kennedy, Cynthia Williams, Isabelle Kalander, John Ledger, and Guillermo Garcia. Special thanks to my family for their help and encouragement.

I

Yes, it's night and another world is rising. Harsh, cynical,
illiterate, amnesiac, revolving without reason . . . Spread out,
flattened, as if perspective and vanishing point had been
abolished . . . And the strange thing is that the living dead
of this world are based on the world before . . .

Philippe Sollers, cited in Jean-Luc Godard,
Histoire(s) du cinéma

If there is to be a livable and shared future on our planet, it will
be a future offline, uncoupled from the world-destroying systems
and operations of 24/7 capitalism. In whatever endures of the
world, the grid, as we live within it today, will have become a
fractured and peripheral part of the ruins on which new communities and interhuman projects may possibly arise. If we're
fortunate, a short-lived digital age will have been overtaken by a
hybrid material culture based on both old and new ways of living
and subsisting cooperatively. Now, amid intensifying social and
environmental breakdown, there is a growing realization that daily
life overshadowed on every level by the internet complex has
crossed a threshold of irreparability and toxicity. More and more

people know or sense this, as they silently experience its damaging consequences. The digital tools and services used by people everywhere are subordinated to the power of transnational corporations, intelligence agencies, criminal cartels, and a sociopathic billionaire elite. For the majority of the earth's population on whom it has been imposed, the internet complex is the implacable engine of addiction, loneliness, false hopes, cruelty, psychosis, indebtedness, squandered life, the corrosion of memory, and social disintegration. All of its touted benefits are rendered irrelevant or secondary by its injurious and sociocidal impacts.

The internet complex has become inseparable from the immense, incalculable scope of 24/7 capitalism and its frenzy of accumulation, extraction, circulation, production, transport, and construction, on a global scale. Behaviors that are inimical to the possibility of a livable and just world are incited in almost every feature of online operations. Fueled by artificially manufactured appetites, the speed and ubiquity of digital networks maximize the incontestable priority of getting, having, coveting, resenting, envying; all of which furthers the deterioration of the world—a world operating without pause, without the possibility of renewal or recovery, choking on its heat and waste. The techno-modernist dream of the planet as a colossal worksite of innovation, invention and material progress continues to attract defenders and apologists. Most of the many projects and industries of "renewable" energy are designed for perpetuating business as usual, for maintaining devastating patterns of consumption, competition, and heightened inequality. Market-driven schemes such as the Green New Deal are absurdly pointless because they do nothing to switch off the expansion of senseless economic activity, the needless uses of electrical power, or the global industries of resource extraction incited by 24/7 capitalism.

This book is aligned with a tradition of social pamphleteering that aims to give voice to what is experienced in common, to what is known or partly known in common but is negated by an overpowering barrage of messages that insist on the unalterability of our administered lives. Many people, on a daily basis, have a visceral grasp of the immiseration of their lives and hopes, but may only have a hesitant awareness of how widely their insights are shared with others. My goal here is not to present a nuanced theoretical analysis, but, in a time of emergency, to affirm the truth of shared understandings and experiences and to insist that forms of radical refusal, rather than adaptation and resignation, are not only possible but necessary. The internet complex functions as an unending announcement of its indispensability and of the insignificance of whatever life remains unassimilable to its protocols. Its omnipresence and embeddedness within almost every sphere of personal and institutional activity makes any notion of its impermanence or post-capitalist marginalization seem unthinkable. But this impression marks a collective failure of imagination, in its passive acceptance of numbing online routines as synonymous with living. It is unthinkable only to the extent that our desires and our bonds with other peoples and species have been wounded and incapacitated.

The philosopher Alain Badiou noted that it is at this point of apparent impossibility that the conditions for insurgency arise: "Emancipatory politics always consist in making seem possible precisely that which, from within the situation, is declared to be impossible."[1] The loudest voices declaring this impossibility are those who benefit from the perpetuation of the way things are, who thrive on the uninterrupted functioning of a capitalist world. These are anyone with a professional, financial, or narcissistic stake in the ascendancy and expansion of the internet complex.

How, they will ask incredulously, could we do without something on which every aspect of financial and economic life depends? Translated, this question is actually: How could we possibly do without one of the core elements of the techno-consumerist culture and economy that has brought life on earth to the edge of collapse? To have a world not dominated by the internet, they will say, would mean changing everything. Yes, precisely.

Any possible path to a survivable planet will be far more wrenching than most recognize or will openly admit. A crucial layer of the struggle for an equitable society in the years ahead is the creation of social and personal arrangements that abandon the dominance of the market and money over our lives together. This means rejecting our digital isolation, reclaiming time as lived time, rediscovering collective needs, and resisting mounting levels of barbarism, including the cruelty and hatred that emanate from online. Equally important is the task of humbly reconnecting with what remains of a world filled with other species and forms of life. There are innumerable ways in which this may occur and, although unheralded, groups and communities in all parts of the planet are moving ahead with some of these restorative endeavors.

However, many of those who understand the urgency of transitioning to some form of eco-socialism or no-growth post-capitalism carelessly presume that the internet and its current applications and services will somehow persist and function as usual in the future, alongside efforts for a habitable planet and for more egalitarian social arrangements. There is an anachronistic misconception that the internet could simply "change hands," as if it were a mid-twentieth-century telecommunications utility, like Western Union or radio and TV stations, which would be put to different uses in a transformed political and economic situation. But the notion that the internet could function independently of the catastrophic operations of global capitalism is one of the stupefying delusions of this moment. They are structurally interwoven, and the dissolution of capitalism, when it happens, will be the end of a market-driven world shaped by the networked technologies of the present. Of course, there will be means of communication in a post-capitalist world, as there always have been in every society, but they will bear little resemblance to the financialized and militarized networks in which we are entangled today. The many digital devices and services we use now are made possible through unending exacerbation of economic inequality and the accelerated disfiguring of the earth's biosphere by resource extraction and needless energy consumption.

Capitalism has always been a conjunction of an abstract system of value and the physical and human externalizations of that system, but, with contemporary digital networks, there is a more complete integration of the two. All of the interconnected phones, laptops, cables, supercomputers, modems, server farms, and cell towers are concretizations of the quantifiable processes of financialized capitalism. The distinction between fixed and circulating capital becomes permanently blurred. Yet many remain attached to the fallacious image of the internet as a free-standing technological assemblage, like a set of tools, and the prevalence of hand-held devices amplifies this illusion.[2] In the early 1970s, the social critic Ivan Illich developed an expansive definition of a tool that included "rationally designed artifacts, productive institutions, and engineered functions." Tools, he wrote, are intrinsically social and he evaluated them in relation to a fundamental opposition: "An individual relates himself in action to his society either through the use of tools he actively masters or by which he is passively acted upon."[3] Illich insisted that people derive happiness and satisfaction through the use of tools that are "least controlled by others," and warned that "the growth of tools beyond a certain point increases regimentation, dependence, exploitation and impotence." In the late 1990s, a few years before his death, he noted the disappearance of technique as a tool that was a means to an end, an instrument through which an individual could invest the world with meaning. Instead, he saw the spread of technologies into whose rules and operations people are integrated. Actions that once were at least partly autonomous now became "system-adaptive" behaviors.[4] Within this historically unprecedented reality, any goals or ends we pursue cease to be ones we have truly chosen.

For all its historical novelty, the internet complex is a magnification and *consolidation* of arrangements that have been operative or partially realized for many years. Hardly monolithic, it's a patchwork of elements from different eras made for a variety of uses, some of which are traceable back to the configurations for financializing flows of electricity devised in the 1880s by Edison and Westinghouse and then usurped by J. P. Morgan. Currently we're witnessing the final act of the mad, incendiary project of a totally wired world, of the reckless belief that 24/7 availability of electrical power to a planet of 8 billion people was achievable without the disastrous consequences now occurring everywhere.

The near instantaneity of the internet's connectivity makes it a fulfillment of Marx's forecast in the 1850s of a global market (*Weltmarkt*). He saw the inevitability of a capitalist unification of the world in which constraints on the speed of circulation and exchange would be progressively diminished through "the annihilation of space by time."[5] Marx also understood that the development of a world market would necessarily lead to "the dissolution of community" and of any social relations independent of the "universalizing tendency of capital." Thus, even if more pervasive now, the isolation associated with digital media is continuous with the social fragmentation produced by institutional and economic forces throughout the twentieth century. Media materialities may change, but the same social experiences of separation, disempowerment, and disruption of community not only persist but intensify. The internet complex quickly became an integral part of neoliberal austerity in its ongoing erosion of civil society and its replacement by monetized, online simulations of social relations. It fosters the belief that we no longer depend on each other, that we are autonomous administrators of our lives, that we can manage our friends in the same way we manage all our online accounts. It also heightens what social theorist Elena Pulcini calls the "narcissistic apathy" of individuals emptied of desire for community and who live in passive conformity with the existing social order.[6]

Ever since the late 1990s we've heard repeatedly that the dominant digital technologies are "here to stay." The master narrative that world civilization has entered "the digital age" promotes the illusion of a historical epoch whose material determinations are beyond any possible intervention or alteration. One result has been the apparent naturalization of the internet which many now assume to be something immutably installed onto the planet. The numerous mystifications of information technologies all conceal their inseparability from the flailing stratagems of a global system in terminal crisis. Little is ever said about how the internet's financialization is intrinsically reliant on a house-of-cards world economy already tottering and threatened further by the plural impacts of planetary warming and infrastructure collapse.

The initial claims of the internet's permanence and inevitability coincided with various "end of history" celebrations, in which free market global capitalism was declared triumphant, without rivals, dominant in perpetuity. Even though, in geopolitical terms, this fiction quickly exploded in the early 2000s, the internet seemed to validate the post-history mirage. It appeared to introduce a uniform, default reality defined by consumption, unhinged from a physical world and its mounting social conflicts and environmental disasters. The advent of social media, with all its apparent opportunities for self-expression, briefly suggested a debased fulfillment of Hegel's horizon of autonomy and recognition for everyone. But now, as a constitutive component of twenty-first-century capitalism, the internet's key functions include the disabling of memory and the absorption of lived temporalities, not ending history but rendering it unreal and incomprehensible. The paralysis of remembrance occurs individually and collectively: we see this in the transience of any "analog" artifacts that are digitized: rather than preservation, their fate is oblivion and loss, noted by no one. In the same way, our own disposability is mirrored in our self-defining devices that quickly become useless pieces of digital trash. The very arrangements that supposedly are "here to stay" depend on the ephemerality, disappearance and forgetting of anything durable or lasting to which there might be shared commitments. In the late 1980s, Guy Debord saw the pervasiveness of these temporalities: "When social significance is attributed only to what is immediate, and to what will be immediate immediately afterwards, always replacing another, identical, immediacy it can be seen that the uses of the media guarantee an eternity of noisy insignificance."[7]

The transformation of the internet from a network used for several decades mainly by military and research institutions into universally available online services in the mid-1990s did not happen simply because of advances in systems engineering. Rather, the shift occurred as an essential part of the massive reorganization of capital flows and the remaking of individuals into "entrepreneurs of their human capital." The widespread introduction of informal, flexible, and decentralized forms of labor were noted by many, but in the early 1980s a smaller number of commentators were able to grasp what was at stake on a deeper level. To take one example, the French economist Jean-Paul de Gaudemar identified a fundamental reconfiguration of capitalism that involved far more than the reorganization of labor and the global dispersion of production. "In effect, we are now living in an age in which it has become clear that capital must henceforth reconquer *the entire social space* from which the previous system had tended to separate it. It must now reincorporate this social body in order more than ever to dominate it."[8] It would have been impossible for anyone in 1980 to foresee the concrete ways in which this reconquering would proceed, or the relentlessness with which it continues, decades later, to subsume more and more layers of lived experience. Countless spheres of the social, with their distinctive autonomies and local textures, have disappeared or been standardized into online simulations. The internet complex is now the comprehensive global apparatus for the dissolution of society.

Beginning in the mid-1990s, the internet complex was promoted as inherently democratic, decentralizing, and anti-hierarchical. It was said to be an unprecedented means for the free exchange of ideas, independent of top-down control, that would level the playing field of media access. But it was none of these. There was a short-lived phase of naïve enthusiasm, similar to the unrealized hopes voiced at the wide availability of cable TV in the 1970s. The narrative now—of an egalitarian technology endangered by monopolistic corporations, the rescinding of net neutrality, and invasions of privacy—is plainly false. There never was or will be a "digital commons." From the start, internet access for a global public was always about the capture of time, about disempowerment and depersonalized connectedness. The only reason the internet seemed "freer" or more open initially was because the projects of financializing and expropriation did not occur all at once and took a number of years to reach an acceleration point in the early 2000s. For transnational corporations, universal access to the internet allowed the reshaping of both work and consumption into 24/7 occupations, freed from the constraints of time or location. This also created vast and interrelated possibilities of monitoring and solicitation of anyone online, and the simultaneous intensification of social privatization. Using the perspective of media historian Harold Innis, the corporate control of digital networks can be understood as a "monopoly of knowledge" which serves the ambitions of a dominant empire or state.[9] While seeming to provide popular or democratic access to information, Innis saw that the larger goal of communication systems throughout history has been to break up local and regional communities by drawing them into larger spheres over which the knowledge monopoly is maintained, thus ensuring cultural and economic domination. Rarely, he noted, did subjugated groups ever effectively appropriate communications media for their own political ends.

By the mid-1990s, the destabilization of work, intensifying economic inequality, dismantling of public services, structural creation of indebtedness, and many other factors required new ways of maintaining political docility. Limitless digital diversions were a deterrent to the rise of anti-systemic mass movements.

Part of the optimistic reception of the internet was the expectation that it would be an indispensable organizing tool for non-mainstream political movements, leveraging the impact of smaller or marginal forms of opposition. In reality, the internet has proven to be a set of arrangements that prevent or close off even the tentative emergence of sustained anti-systemic organizing and action. Certainly, the internet can function instrumentally transmitting information to large numbers of recipients, for example, in aid of short-term, single-issue mobilization, often linked to identity politics, "color revolutions," climate marches, or transient expressions of outrage. Also, it should be remembered that broad-based radical movements and far larger mass mobilizations were achieved in the 1960s and early '70s without any fetishization of the material means used for organizing.

Accounts of the internet as an egalitarian, horizontal field of "public spheres" have deleted any class-based language or advocacy of class struggle at a historical moment when class antagonisms are as acute as ever. Indeed, the internet complex has never been deployed with even minor success in furthering an anti-capitalist or anti-war agenda. It disperses the disempowered into a cafeteria of separate identities, sects, and interests and is especially effective at solidifying reactionary group formations. The insularity it produces becomes an incubator of particularisms, racisms, and neo-fascisms. Identity politics, as Nancy Fraser and others have argued, has been crucial to the strategies of "progressive" neoliberal elites: to ensure that a potentially powerful majority cannot recognize itself, being split into separate and competing factions from which a handful of representatives are allowed conspicuous entry into the meritocracy.[10] The internet carries this strategy of highlighting diversity and encouraging compartmentalization to a new level of effectiveness. At the same time, the fact that social media can circulate only the most easily packaged ideas dilutes and domesticates potentially radical or insurgent programs, especially those which do not produce immediate results, or which might require long-term engagement. Communication theorists have identified ways in which forms of media become "steering mechanisms" serving to limit, shape or redirect public debate. The internet has become the most infinitely nuanced and powerful of such steering mechanisms in the history of mass media. It would be difficult to find an ongoing "conversation" that has not been shaped by increasingly efficient mechanisms for orienting online exchanges and intervening in their content.

Numerous activist groups have recognized the trap of social media after experiencing forms of sabotage, disruption, and surveillance, as well as a weakening of trust and camaraderie among real world communities of face-to-face participants. To take one of many examples, the Florida group Dream Defenders, formed in the aftermath of the 2012 murder of Trayvon Martin, suspended and subsequently marginalized their use of social media because of its deleterious impact on their organization and its goals. In the words of one of their organizers:

> All the fighting that happens on social media is indicative of the fact that people really don't know each other. Social media provides the illusion of deep relationships. So long as people don't really know each other, the work is never going to go that far. This is doing the work of COINTELPRO in the sense that you see people calling each other out online, and you see all these rifts being created. Social media is doing that to us. Stepping back from all that is really important right now. We're in a really critical time where all of this could

actually kill the movement . . . Being off social media is an opportunity for us to really understand how it's impacting us, how it's being used to manipulate us by our oppressor.[11]

An electoral politics based around involving people through internet solicitation, as some center-left parties in Europe have attempted, inevitably produces a de-politicization of those whose participation is the ostensible goal. "Politics" becomes continuous with the same gestures and keystrokes, the same recourse to surveys and opinion polls that strengthen one's integration into the routines of consumerism and self-administration. The result is one step forward, three steps back. Unless the difficult task of creating new cooperative and communal forms of living becomes a political priority, all kinds of online activism will continue to occur innocuously, without attaining any radical or foundational changes. Demonstrations, protests, marches take place but, simultaneously, there is a re-immersion in the atomizing separation of digital life. The bonds that seem to have blossomed in the midst of action evaporate. Even in the actual event of marches, occupations, liberated zones, and mobilizations of all kinds, group solidarity is reduced by the critical mass of individuals who are also elsewhere, clinging to their devices and to the self-promotional resources of social media.

Despite a small uptrend in openness to the possibilities of socialism in the US, it has mainly led to debate about candidates for electoral office and stand-alone economic initiatives. Missing has been the understanding that socialism cannot simply be implemented on the level of governmentality and economic policies but that, more importantly, building toward it requires changes in consciousness and everyday activity. In the late nineteenth and early twentieth centuries, many anarcho-socialists practiced ways of living and connecting with others that would prefigure or anticipate a larger social world of mutual support. During those years, especially in Europe, the flourishing of communal groups and workers' organizations provided foundations for de-privatized forms of coexistence and sharing of resources. For the German revolutionary Gustav Landauer, "socialism is the continual becoming of community in humankind"; it is action that carries its ends within itself.[12] The capitalist state, he wrote, "is a condition, a certain relationship between human beings, a mode of behavior; we destroy it by contracting other relationships, by behaving differently."[13] Landauer recognized the necessity of becoming new kinds of subjects, of making the difficult transition to prioritizing responsibility to others over the mirage of individual autonomy. Such a transition will never happen online: the internet overwhelmingly produces self-interested subjectivities incapable of imagining goals or outcomes other than private, individual ones. However, for the minority committed to social change, the idea of a radical transformation to modes of living is rarely prioritized over the sheltered habituations of online activity. As long as one panics at the idea of sharing and cooperating with others as a way of life, one is incapable of revolt and remains dependent on existing institutions. The truth is irrefutable: there are no revolutionary subjects on social media.

The debacle is the folly of pursuing systemic change through the apparatuses that guarantee submission to the givens and rules imposed by those in power. Anyone inculcated with some of the political platitudes of postmodernism would insist the opposite is true, that one can never occupy a position outside of the "meshes of power," a diffuse power that extends everywhere and cannot be confronted. For many critics and academics, such a notion became a convenient basis for dismissing the possibility of revolt or militancy as outdated and unfashionable. Now, the internet complex, with all its tools for individual advancement and branding, is the new, self-serving delusion of the "meshes of power" from which use of ever-changing social media platforms can masquerade as opposition or resistance.

The analysis by the Retort Collective in their 2004 book, *Afflicted Powers*, remains acutely relevant today, especially their discussion of the role of mass media in the fostering of obedience and apathy in the aftermath of 9/11. For these writers, the most significant feature of globalization is planet-wide militarization and they described how the strategy of "permanent war" always seeks to normalize itself, to become unnoticed through familiarity and ubiquity. An unending sequence of military interventions had to be represented "as an unexceptional part of the state's external political life" in order to ensure the docility of domestic populations.[14] Thus, they indicated the role of media apparatuses in fostering a callous unconcern with civilian casualties occurring in distant locations. Put simply, war facilitates the plunder of resources, the securing of markets and the creation of cheap and exploitable labor. The Retort writers identified a two-pronged strategy of military intervention to produce failed states and regional instabilities in the periphery and using other less violent methods to promote disinterested citizenship and compliant consumers in the core.

No doubt they would have noted that, since the economic collapse of 2008, forms of state terror and economic immiseration have been brought home for deployment against many domestic communities and populations. In addition, it's possible now to recognize other features of that post-9/11 moment which would not have been evident at the time. The strengthening of a permanent warfare state coincided with the installation and mass adoption of Web 2.0. Counterintuitively, a configuration that supported user-generated content and supposedly enabled a participatory internet culture was a factor in furthering the normalization of war and its invisibility to those millions of people cocooned online. Equally significant is the mass indifference to the quasi-permanent installation of US military infrastructure across the entire planet. Except for a small number of activists, there is a broad refusal to even acknowledge the activities of "the single largest developer, landowner, equipment contractor and energy consumer in the world."[15] Mass mobilizations against imperial wars had exerted at least a partial restraint on US foreign interventions, but the internet quickly contributed to the marginalization of resistance following the global protests in February 2003 against the impending invasion of Iraq. The sustained kind of struggle and solidarities demanded by an anti-war or anti-imperialist movement are irreconcilable with the temporalities and vacant forms of attentiveness that accompany the proliferation of social media.

The current indifference to US military interventions and to the looting of resources in the Global South must be viewed against the very different trajectory of international activism in the years 1994–2001. From the first Zapatista uprising to the anti-WTO demonstrations in Genoa, the anti-globalization movements were motivated by a conviction that defeating neoliberal capitalism had to be the overriding objective and the foundation for local or more circumscribed struggles. A 1998 manifesto of People's Global Action expressed this priority: "We have to start aiming at the head; we have been militants fighting against nuclear power, against homelessness, against sexism— different tentacles of the monster. But you are never really going to do it that way, you have to aim at the head."[16] The momentum generated by the events of Seattle, Genoa, and elsewhere was in part derailed by the 9/11-related cancellation of IMF/World Bank meetings in Washington DC scheduled for late September 2001. Now, twenty years later, in a changed world, that earlier focus and strategic clarity of global anti-capitalist movements continue to be dispersed into a medley of particularized grievances. In a recent look back at the 1999 anti-capitalist demonstrations in Seattle, the anarchist activist Chris Dixon detailed the months of collective organizing ahead of the WTO meetings, involving thousands of people who "went into high schools, churches, labor councils, neighborhood associations, workplaces and universities" to form affinity groups and to test out creative forms of direct democracy in a community-based struggle. His account is, perhaps unintentionally, a harsh verdict on the shallowness and inadequacy of activism based on internet and social media strategies.

Near the end of his life, in 2007, Jean Baudrillard observed that the logic of Western modernity required that it be imposed on the entire world, that no peoples or places should escape its demands. The West, he writes, exports its economic and cultural models everywhere in the name of universality but it is a nulli-fying universality, emptied of any truths, leaving in its wake all that has been de-sacralized, unveiled, objectified, financialized. It is a challenge to the rest of the world "to debase themselves in their turn, to deny their own values . . . to sacrifice everything by which a human being or a culture has some value in its own eyes."[17] But what Baudrillard identifies here was well underway much earlier, as Aimé Césaire's 1955 account of European colo-nization makes clear: "They talk to me about progress, diseases cured, highways built, improved standards of living. *I* am talking about societies drained of their essence, cultures trampled underfoot, institutions undermined, lands confiscated, religions smashed, magnificent artistic creations destroyed, extraordinary *possibilities* wiped out."[18]

The social atomization of the internet reproduces something intrinsically American in its relentless maximization of acquisitiveness, in the illusory independence it seems to promise the user and its capacity for one-way communication, freed up from dialogue or reciprocity, and detached from a physical place. As Bernard Stiegler and others have argued, the internet complex incarnates a specifically American model of technological consumption to which there has been little or no resistance in Europe and elsewhere, resulting in the liquidation of regional or national cultures.[19] For Stiegler, one of the innovations exported by the US is technology for "the mass production of behavior" and for a hyper-synchronization of consciousness which has led to "the decomposition of the social as such." The "hegemonic rule of the market," in which calculation and computation are extended into every area of life, makes it impossible for an individual to love oneself or love others or to have any desire for the future.[20]

All the seemingly altruistic fervor about overcoming "the digital divide" continues to be a unified campaign by corporate interests to require digital compliance everywhere, including the use of computer-based learning in schools for even the youngest of students. The suggestion has been that people without broadband access are living in a condition of deprivation, cut off from the possibility of upward mobility, career opportunities and cultural enrichment. However, the primary goal of the most powerful stakeholders is the eventual transformation of everyone into captive and obedient consumers of their products and service. The unspoken truth is that as internet access and use expands, economic inequality is heightened, not diminished. "Tech literacy" is a euphemism for shopping, gaming, binge watching and other monetized and addictive behaviors. Wealthy, cynical power brokers like Nicholas Negroponte, founder of MIT Media Lab, pontificate about making internet access a "human right" while corporate-friendly agendas promote "a laptop for every child," despite the unmitigated failures of computer-based education in elementary schools. However, the juggernaut of high-tech companies marketing their products and services in the Global South and elsewhere has had more injurious consequences. The violent processes of Western modernization have always targeted the survival of local or regional singularities. In nations or areas in which traditional or indigenous solidarities persist, the internet complex becomes a new techno-colonization, ripping apart long-standing forms of social cohesion. Now, even its partial installation introduces another layer of homogenization, but this time at the level of consciousness.

The reality of intensifying global polarization and inequality is continually disguised by mainstream media fabrications of a planet happily coming closer together through the technology we share. Thus we are told how First Nations fishermen in Labrador use GPS software to route their boats, how indigenous communities in Australia use Facebook "to tell their stories," how textile artists in Zimbabwe sell their goods on Etsy and eBay, and how MOOCs (massive open online courses) are bringing enlightenment and prosperity to North Africa and the Middle East. Implicit in these accounts is that the "civilizing" impact of the internet will lift the disadvantaged out of their technological limitations, allowing them to become "like us." Such journalism

is not just feel-good, we-are-the-world reassurance that all is
heading in the right direction. It's also a disclosure of the deep-
er-rooted, colonizing premise that the poor regions of the
periphery desire and welcome the adoption of Western technology, including social media, and that they will necessarily
benefit from its implantation. For political theorist Samir Amin,
this is the legacy of Eurocentrism at its worst—that is, of capitalism putting forward a model of material abundance that is
structurally impossible to achieve, and is never in fact its actual
goal. Once the lure of Western modernization is accepted, what
follows only perpetuates and intensifies unequal relations. As
Enrique Dussel and others have argued, we are now in the last
stages, not just of capitalism, but of the entire European
world-system that has been in place for nearly 500 years, based
on the exploitation and murder of non-European peoples and
the natural world. The internet complex, as the new modality
of planetary administration, is an indispensable part of the defens-
ive strategy to maintain the world system, to resist decolonization
and de-Westernization. Its global availability makes it an essential part of all the economic and military efforts to counter the
hard realities of geography, in which North America is on the
literal and symbolic periphery of an emerging post-Western
planet. As Dussel insists, the defeat of this world-system with
its threat to the survival of all life is now the single greatest task
of humanity.[21]

Capitalism's unlivable temporalities infuse the conditions of
working and living together with desperation and hopelessness.
Everything necessary for a minimal sense of stability, whether
jobs, homes, communities or health care is, by design, always on
the edge of being discarded, downsized, foreclosed, demolished.
This where the sociopathology of capitalism becomes most

virulent. Franco Berardi and others have discussed how neo-liberalism and its technological armature produce new manifestations of psychosis on a global scale. For Berardi, we're living in a time of "annihilating nihilism," in which the disintegration of long-standing forms of social solidarity are inseparable from epidemics of depression, addiction, and suicide.[22] The anger, the cruelty, and the avowals of victimhood that pervade the internet continue to spill out into real space in ever more frequent episodes of mass violence. Especially in the US, an underlying creed of resentment, individualism, and freedom from responsibility to others begets its now familiar monsters. Here, alongside all the commodities we are exhorted to covet, one product stands apart: the gun. The gun symbolically, and too often in actuality, redeems the hollowness of a material culture that produces powerlessness and disappointment. A gun does not wear out and rarely needs repair. For many, it is the reassuring inverse of all the shoddy objects and broken relationships that pass in and out of one's life. Most of all, the gun in its inherent lethality becomes the last guarantee of a society of equals and the frightful specter of a vanished individual agency.

In the 1970s, madness was often understood as a condition which mirrored the dislocations of capitalism but was simultaneously a delirium of interruption, of escape that held at least some radical potential, as Deleuze and Guattari argued in *Anti-Oedipus*. We see this mapped out in 1970s fictions such as Marge Piercy's *Woman on the Edge of Time*, Doris Lessing's *Briefing for a Descent into Hell* and Leslie Silko's *Ceremony*, where these authors explore how madness instigates the breakouts, the departures to other experiences of time and desire, and to rediscoveries of community. Now, four decades later, capitalism's harsh levelings and liquidations are more invasive and widespread than in the 1970s. Madness finds fewer pathways to flight or breakout to an elsewhere. The involuntary immersion in 24/7 temporalities heightens a pervasive condition of quasi-psychosis bereft of anything fugitive or nomadic. Ludwig Binswanger, writing in the 1950s, outlined it as follows: "What is renounced is life as independent autonomous selfhood. The subject thus surrenders itself over to existential powers alien to itself."[23] In this account, schizophrenia is a withdrawal from being-in-the-world, from life as something lived communally, and is experienced as a condition in which "one's existence is worn away, as though by friction." For Deleuze and Guattari, the schizo is "first of all, the one who can no longer bear '*all that*': money, the stock market, values, morals, homelands, religions."[24] Now, decades later, "all that" includes an obligatory digital identity, passwords, 24/7 engagement with online media and the monetization of all aspects of working or living. The madness is compounded by repeated declarations by seemingly knowledgeable voices that this is all "here to stay," that there is no other way to live.

Although some of the celebratory fabrications about cyberspace are still given lip service, it's clear that the internet never was a collective apparatus that could dismantle hierarchical institutions, reconfigure power relations, and enable a plurality of once marginal voices to be heard and empowered. With those illusions abandoned, the broad acceptance of present arrangements as necessary and inevitable comes as much from resignation and fatigue as from the impossibility of life-affirming and non-financialized uses of the internet complex. In the 1990s, some argued that, amid the precarious circumstances of work and life within the global economy, there was enormous insurgent potential latent within the communicative and information technologies immediately at hand. Some claimed that mobile labor and fragmented forms of work, at least in principle, could be the basis for "a general creativity" and even resistance that might disturb existing political relations. This hope was based on the supposition that individual activity within networks necessarily interacted or converged with the work of many others. There was anticipation that collaborative exchanges and shared inventiveness might overcome the disconnectedness that had long been part of the industrial division of labor, and might have the potential to develop into new forms of political struggle.

But such optimistic speculation was based on a model of the workplace and on a notion of "immaterial labor" that bore little resemblance to the actual circumstances of workers as austerity measures intensified. Now, two decades later, the reality of low-wage labor using digital technology is of repetitive and physically enervating tasks, subject to harsh time-management and productivity surveillance. The prospect of "cooperative networks" or online "peer to peer" exchanges leading to effective political agency has given way to the pervasive realities of workplace isolation, despair, and the threat of disposability. Gig economy workers have little to share with each other but their destitution and exhaustion. Since the 1990s, there has been a further breakdown of separations between work time and non-work time, between public and private time, making the creation of political or civic community difficult or impossible to achieve. Portions of life that had once been demarcated as private or personal become an unending chain of online obligations that are in force at all waking hours. Edward Snowden's spurious claim that network technology is "the great equalizer" perpetuates an elitist hacker fantasy of covert empowerment that has little relevance to most people's lives or to the building of mass movements and new communities. The internet complex is obviously fraught with social contradictions but there is no way a dialectical analysis can conjure it into a locus or set of tools for class struggle. To suggest that the internet is where indigenous peoples, stateless immigrants, the unemployed and impoverished, and the incarcerated should contest their marginalization and disposability is not just wrong but malevolently irresponsible.

Proponents of modernization and development in the twentieth century were strident champions of "massification," whether of society, culture, or business. Advocates of small, human-scale social formations or undertakings were ridiculed as nostalgic or reactionary. The exalting of the mass has always been about the financialization of large demographics, although its relocation from the physical space of the crowd and of production to the internet has had new affective consequences. The crushing asymmetries of scale between an individual person and global networks disfigure any non-quantified notions of importance or value. Each of us is demeaned by the veneration of statistics—followers, clicks, likes, hits, views, shares, dollars—that, fabricated or not, are an ongoing rebuke to one's self-belief. When the availability of images and information is infinite, there is a fatal scattering of anything held in common and the relationships that make possible a society are dissolved. The phenomenon of something trending or going viral is a mass surge of a vague and amorphous unanimity, of an irresistible but vacuous assent to some trivia or pseudo-outrage which is quickly forgotten and leaves no trace. Drained of intentionality, it becomes a monstrous and disempowering simulation of a collective pronouncement. The philosopher Roberto Unger has argued that "belittlement" is the inevitable lot of human beings in a social world, where most people experience a lifelong gap between their own desires and hopes and the extent to which these are ever recognized or fulfilled by society. The immeasurable dimensions of the internet, however, become a new intensification of "belittlement" in the humiliating effacement of any individual gesture of self-affirmation. In seeking antidotes to belittlement, Unger observes that we fall into "the sleepwalking of compromise, conformity and the petrified self. We seize upon devices and stratagems that divide and enslave us under the pretext of empowering us."[25]

From the beginning, the social and commercial segments of the internet have provided innumerable tools for deception and manipulation. An array of platforms and applications not only enable but reward sociopathic behavior. The internet has bred a hybrid class of striving professionals and their many emulators for whom friendship, caring, and honesty are impediments to maximizing the enriching potential of online enterprise. At its most basic, the "sociopathic" denotes what is *anti-social* or injurious to the existence of a society and the depersonalization of most online interactions fuels the sociopath's remorselessness, selfishness and lack of empathy. One of the factors in the normalization of the internet complex was the promotion of a spatial model in which the billions of "surface crawlers" (people who use social media, Netflix, Amazon) are distanced from the "deep web" or the "dark corners" of the internet. But there is no separation or insulation from the pernicious objectives of the most powerful actors online. Once human communication becomes lodged in a system customized to the priorities of global corporations, the military, intelligence agencies, criminal cartels, sex traffickers, and depraved operators of all kinds, there is no more accountability to anyone or anything. It is the quintessential unregulated free market of late capitalism. The internet

complex is uniformly and unalterably "dark" because the nihilistic maxim, "everything is permitted," has been refashioned into
the more corrupt form of "everything is permitted, as long as it
can be monetized and made available on demand." The pathology of the internet is not what is transacted in its less accessible
circuitry but rather in the naturalization of how our needs,
desires, and affections are diverted or severed from a commitment
to care for a world lived in common with others. The temporalities and values of an on-demand world are unlivable and the
appetites incited are terminally insatiable.

As recently as the late twentieth century, it was still plausible
to imagine global elites acting, in limited ways, on the basis of
long-term consequences and class self-interest, even if their policies involved crimes against humanity. In her 1999 book, *The
Lugano Report*, Susan George presented a chilling parafiction of
financiers and corporate strategists concocting policies to ensure
the survival of capitalism and the perpetual rule of the billionaire
class. George simulated a working paper for a Davos-like summit
meeting which identified the trends and policies that would
safeguard corporate-led globalization and accumulation. The
scandal of *The Lugano Report* was its undisguised contention that
capitalism's long-term prospects depend on a drastic reduction
in world population (i.e., the deaths of a few billion human
beings). Without such a decrease, it concludes, the ensuing social
unrest, resource scarcity and other instabilities will reach unman-
ageable levels. "We cannot both sustain the liberal, free market
system and simultaneously continue to tolerate the presence of
superfluous, unproductive billions."[26] But this was not a Malthu-
sian observation, for the report details the currently existing
policies through which mass extermination is achievable. Some
of these are political and financial measures to cause famine,

epidemics, protracted and murderous intra-ethnic conflicts, environmental blight, sterilization programs, and the many deadly consequences of manufactured "failed states." Since the book's publication, the coalescence of the actual forms of violence it outlined have led to over 8 million deaths in the Congo alone, while the death and ruination there and in many other regions continues.

Now, however, with the post-2008 global economy on life support, with the growth of corrupt autocratic regimes and cartel states, and with the looming imponderables of the climate crisis, long-term calculation by powerful interests has given way to short-term forms of enrichment. This is casino capitalism at midnight, when the winning players begin to cash in their chips. Because the global economy no longer has any long-term prospects, one, last, mad spree of plunder is now ongoing all over the planet. Fracking, mountain-top removal mining, rainforest clear-cutting for biofuel farming, offshore drilling, wilderness despoliation proceed alongside the ravaging and looting of social resources, the expropriation of the remaining fragments of a commons, whether drinking water, wilderness or city parks. It's like a new version of the 1960s TV game show *Supermarket Sweep*, where contestants were given a shopping cart and a time limit within which they could frantically grab anything of value in the store.

As many have noted, the falsifications of "the digital age" have been so successfully inculcated that, despite direct evidence to the contrary, there is a pervasive imaginary of the dematerialized status of digital technology. Material and environmental realities are conveniently veiled by miniaturization, the apparent intangibility of wireless setups, the placelessness of data, and terms like "virtual" or "cloud." One of the many phenomena refuting these illusions is the ceaseless construction of new data centers and server farms to manage the massive increase in data production. These sprawling single-story structures have staggering energy requirements and generate levels of heat damaging to micro-circuitry, which must be cooled at each unit using millions of gallons of water each day. At current exponential rates of data growth, the required number of server farms fifty years from now would cover vast areas of the land surface of the continental US and other regions. The mythologies of a post-industrial information economy also obscure the persistence of earlier modes of production within the current scramble for resources essential to high-tech weaponry, communication networks, consumer technology products, solar and wind energy systems and much else. Violence to both people and their lands defines these imperial and neocolonial operations, as it has for several centuries. The very possibility of a "digital age" requires the expansion of these destructive industrial practices to world-vanquishing extremes.

Using the historical framework of Lewis Mumford, our technological present is fully dependent on a *paleotechnic* paradigm of resource extraction, specifically the activities of mining and drilling into the earth and laying waste to the land. As he outlined it, the paleotechnic era began in Europe after 1750, in North America around 1850, and continued to define much of the world when he was writing in the 1930s. Equally important for Mumford were the institutional forms of discipline and subjugation needed to carry out these large-scale projects. He understood that the regimentation and debasement of workers' lives and the industrial degradation of the environment were related forms of oppression. For Mumford, the consequences of what he appropriately termed "carboniferous capitalism" included the wounding of sensory and perceptual experience amid the interconnected requirements of war and industrial production. A condition of partial anesthesia became necessary for survival.

The state of Paleotechnic society may be described as one of wardom. Its typical organs, from mine to factory, from blast furnace to slum, from slum to battlefield, were at the service of death: competition, struggle for existence, domination and submission, extinction. With war at once the main stimulus and underlying basis of this society, the normal motives and reactions of human beings were narrowed down to the fear of poverty, the fear of unemployment, the fear of losing class status, the fear of starvation, the fear of annihilation . . . The mine and the battlefield underlay all paleotechnic activities, and the practices they stimulated led to the widespread exploitation of fear.[27]

Mumford tempered his pessimism in the 1930s with the anticipation that a new, enlightened technological era might supplant these depredations. He had erroneous expectations that electronics, lightweight materials and telecommunications would usher in a Neotechnic era, in which meeting social and environmental needs would become priorities. But, by the 1960s, Mumford had abandoned this hopeful vision as he witnessed the establishment of "a state of permanent war" and the advent of more extreme forms of ecological damage. The technologies he had imagined as possible means of societal transformation had become integrated into the operations of multinational corporations and the military. The mechanized slaughter by US forces in Vietnam and Cambodia was only one part of his realization that "paleotechnic ideals still largely dominate the consciousness and politics of the Western world."

Nothing better epitomizes the grim persistence of those ideals than the worldwide expansion of open pit mining, mining on a scale of magnitude and savagery that dwarfs comparable activity during the so-called Industrial Revolution or during the twentieth century. At present, there are over 500,000 active quarries and pits, employing over 45 million people, unearthing minerals as well as the sand and gravel needed for new roads and megacities. The Grasberg mine in the Indonesian province of Papua, one of the world's largest and most profitable, is exemplary: the excavated crater measures 12 square miles, and over 700,000 tons of tailings are dumped into local rivers every week. It employs 23,000 workers who earn less than $1.50 an hour. Since the 1990s, several thousand Papuan separatist rebels, striking mine workers and environmentalists have been killed by private security forces. Most of the extensive highland and rainforest regions have been irreversibly contaminated by toxic runoff. All of this is to meet the demand for copper by electronics manufacturers, especially for core components of the Green New Deal: solar panels, wind turbines, electric vehicles, but also for the chips in supercomputers, and all the wiring in "smart" homes powered by the Internet of Things. Copper cable is still the preferred electrical conductor for industrial-scale power generation and transmission and for most telecommunications. The owner of the Grasberg mine, Freeport-McMoRan, manages dozens of comparably destructive mines all over the planet, including in Peru, Chile, Bolivia, Mauritania, South Africa, Zambia, and New Mexico. The operations of hundreds of other companies looting lithium for electric vehicle batteries, neodymium for wind turbines, coltan for Predator drones, nickel, molybdenum and other elements for digital devices and networks, multiply this immeasurable scale of sociocidal extraction, especially in the Global South. In Peru, a Chinese company is in a decades-long process of literally levelling 15,000 ft Mt. Toromocho to recover several billion tons of minerals—another small instance of the capitalist cannibalization of the planet in the service of prolonging the imploding "digital age." The toxic methods of removing rare metals from mined ore cause irremediable harm to land, water, and human lives; and yet most smartphone owners, social media users and Netflix addicts in the US have no idea of where Papua or Peru are and no interest in the lives of their peoples. The advocates of green capitalism and "renewables" offer fraudulent assurances that, with oversight, resource extraction could be done without destroying habitats, ecosystems and human communities, but they know this will never happen. History has conclusively shown capitalism to be irreconcilable with conservation or preservation of any kind. As heat energy diffuses throughout the biosphere to life-extinguishing levels, it's important to state the obvious: these minerals must stay in the ground and the urgent task is the radical scaling down of a need for unlimited 24/7 energy and for all the unnecessary, disposable products and services that warp our lives and poison the earth.

One of the defining currents of Western thought is an objectification of nature that cuts us off from our inherence in the limitless creativity and variability of the physical world. Carolyn Merchant, Vandana Shiva, Silvia Federici, and many others have shown how the modern project of domination *over* nature begins in the sixteenth century.[28] Merchant provides one of the clearest accounts of how animistic and organic assumptions about the cosmos were replaced by a view of nature "as a system of dead, inert particles moved by external rather than inherent forces." She describes how new institutional and juridical forms of patriarchy and misogyny grew out of the rejection of a nurturing and vitalistic understanding of nature and the restructuring of reality around the metaphor of the machine. For Philippe Descola, the idea of a categorical separation between nature and humanity gained acceptance in early modern Europe and was reinforced by a belief in "a universal human tendency to overcome natural constraints and instinctive forces."[29] Thus, social customs and behaviors that derived from an interlacing of the human with animals, insects, plants, forests, rivers were eliminated or marginalized. A lifeworld whose social rhythms were originally shaped by the alteration of the seasons, phases of the moon, migration of birds, the oscillation of day and night, of sleep and waking, the sequence of festivals, nonetheless left its traces on the seemingly insignificant activities of everyday life. It was these endlessly variegated cycles that nourished the shared commitments and forms of association in pre-modern cultures, but by the middle of the nineteenth century only fragments of that lifeworld survived. During the twentieth century, the tradition-based reservoirs of knowledge, moral conviction and individual competence were effectively nullified in the developed world by an onslaught of rationalizing forces.[30] At the same time, there was a pervasive acceptance, either celebratory or regretful, that a disenchanted world was the inevitable consequence of Enlightenment and material progress. Now, however, it is inescapably evident that Western modernization and its disenchantment of the world has brought us to the edge of global catastrophe and extinction.[31] The great heresy for the religions of techno-modernism and Western science is to affirm that the world is animate and that all livings things are interconnected and interdependent. An *animate* world, as the etymology of the word suggests, is one that breathes, that unites everything in it with the rhythmic pulse of a world-soul.

In retrospect, a fateful feature of the anti-systemic struggles of the 1960s was the absence of a radical environmental component of the critiques of imperialism, colonialism and capitalism. There were numerous, ground-breaking accounts of the urgency of ecological crisis throughout the 1960s, but this work remained largely unnoted or peripheral for those in liberation, anti-war and student movements.[32] In 1970, Guy Debord wrote that capitalism's destruction of the environment was the most pressing issue for the very survival of life, but readers and commentators generally ignored this important element of his work. In his essay *A Sick Planet*, he showed that the consequences of capitalist development were reaching lethal and terminal levels but also indicated how this disaster is reabsorbed into images and language affirming the ability of existing institutions to solve or mitigate the crisis.[33] When Debord reclaimed the historical slogan "Revolution or Death," this time the life and death at stake were not of individuals or social movements but of the entire planet.

Unfortunately, many on the left in the early 1970s regarded any attention to environmental issues as a diversion from the anti-war and liberation struggles of the time. The first Earth Day on April 22, 1970, with its dubious institutional sponsorship, was rendered irrelevant several weeks later when student protesters were killed by National Guard and police at Kent State and Jackson State. The skepticism of activists was not without some justification, but, more crucially, the radical left was unable to grasp how the Vietnam War manifested the biocide at the heart of Western imperialism. A unique historical opportunity to merge an eco-socialist critique of capitalism with already mobilized mass movements was tragically lost. And, by the 1980s, when some former leftists had morphed into postmodernists and post-structuralists, the patronizing disdain for anyone who talked about nature or environmentalism was all-pervasive. A memorable marker of the critical oblivion of that time was Fredric Jameson's 1991 ill-considered declaration, on the first page of his celebrated tome: "Postmodernism is what you have when the modernization process is complete and nature is gone for good."[34] To foreground issues of animal rights, protection of indigenous peoples, preservation of rainforests or endangered species was to be dismissed as nostalgic and naïve: new effects of power and commodification were everywhere, it was asserted, and there was nothing beyond or "outside" of them. The failings of that phase of trans-Atlantic intellectual culture are evident in Jacques Derrida's *Specters of Marx* (1993), where he listed "the ten plagues of the new world order" of neoliberalism.[35] These included unemployment, debt, arms trafficking, interethnic wars, criminal cartel states, but not a hint of impending ecological catastrophe or of capitalism's contribution to mass extinctions and the collapse of ecosystems. For some deconstructionists, environmental crisis was simply a rhetorical confusion: to be concerned about "pollution" was to be trapped in a binary in which "purity" was the reciprocal term.

Modern industrial civilization is on the brink of setting the world on fire. The eradication of social formations and communities is intertwined with the extinguishing of the living earth-system on which a human commons depends. We're now experiencing capitalism in its terminal, scorched earth phase. In a military context, this meant the destruction of life-essential resources to deny them to a defeated population or to an advancing army. In a more general sense, a scorched earth is one on which thriving regions have been reduced to a state of barrenness and have lost their capacity for regeneration. It is a parched earth deprived of water, its rivers and aquifers poisoned, air polluted and soils afflicted by drought and chemical agriculture. Scorched earth capitalism destroys whatever allows groups and communities to pursue modes of self-sufficient subsistence, of self-governance or of mutual support. This occurs with extreme violence in the Global South where extraction, deforestation, and toxic dumping create uninhabitable wastelands, and cities in which the poor become desperate, internal exiles. The calculated maintenance of low-level warfare or conflicts between drug cartels ensures the disappearance of anything that once resembled civil society. It's clear now that capitalism will never achieve the complete subsumption of life, still foreseen by some. However, it is proving more than capable of the mutilation and extermination of everything that sustains life.

Etymologically, undercurrents of the word scorch go back to the Old French *escorchier*, which means to flay or to strip the skin off a body, rendering it fatally exposed. The flaying of the earth's life-giving and protective layerings accelerates every month, exemplified by the burning of the Amazon forests, the bleaching of coral reefs, the strangling of great rivers with hydro-electric dams, and the massive loss of temperate grasslands. Directly related is one of the enduring meanings of the English verb *scorch*: to burn a surface to the point that its color and texture are singed and shriveled. This is the present we inhabit now—a bleak world nearly divested of its color, of the impalpable but vivid singularity which gives meaning to our lives. Color is the non-quantifiable texture of our loves and hopes, of human connectedness to each other and to the earth; but it is eroded by the unending leveling and homogenization of experience. In a world saturated with violence and casual cruelty, most living and nascent forms of creativity and compassion are defenseless.

John Ruskin, for whom attunement to the colors of the world
was a moral imperative, provides an early, visionary evocation of
a scorched earth marked by the savagery of modern warfare
and the terrible human costs of factory labor. Industrialization and
militarization were for him "the European death of the nineteenth century." Writing around 1860, his image of this death
is an earth lit by an intolerable brightness that cannot be shut
off: "Full shone now its awful globe, one pallid charnel-house—a
ball strewn bright with human ashes, glaring in poised sway
beneath the sun, all blinding-white with death from pole to
pole—death, not of myriads of poor bodies only, but of will,
and mercy, and conscience; death, not once inflicted on the flesh
but daily fastening on the spirit."[36]

Rosa Luxemburg (who, like Ruskin, admired the paintings of
Turner) provided a larger historical framework for understanding
the cataclysm of capitalism. For her, it was a uniquely European
invention, originating in the initial projects of colonization in
the sixteenth century. She poses as axiomatic that "capital must
begin by planning for the comprehensive destruction and annihilation of all the non-capitalist social units which obstruct its
development."[37] In her account, derived from Marx, she contrasts
the violence of European states with numerous earlier instances
of invasion and despotic occupation in Asia and the Near East.
These conquests may have brutally pursued the aim of domination and exploitation but, she insists, "none was interested in
completely robbing the people of their productive forces or in
destroying their social organization." In spite of taxation and
oppression of various kinds, peasants and artisans nonetheless
were able to continue with their age-old patterns of subsistence,
and "the traditional structure" of their lives endured. In contrast,
premodern agrarian societies are helpless in the face of what she

memorably calls "the whiff of death from European capitalism." It produces the collapse of the whole social structure, "tearing apart all traditional bonds and transforming the society in a short period of time into a shapeless pile of rubble."[38] The displaced and dispossessed faced extermination, slavery, or the basest forms of wage labor. Luxemburg astutely notes how capitalist Europe is the first place where "the uncertainty of social existence" and the precariousness of life and work is a fundamental systemic goal, not a secondary by-product.

The language used here recalls how Karl Polanyi, in the early 1940s, characterized the consequences of an unrestrained free market: if left unchecked it would "annihilate the human and natural substance of society; it would physically destroy man and transform his surroundings into wilderness."[39] Although Polanyi was writing at a moment when it appeared that state-sponsored reforms and interventions might restrain the worst effects of free markets, he nonetheless provided a dire survey of the lifeworld that had been a casualty of capitalism in the nineteenth century: "the destruction of family life, the devastation of neighborhoods, the denudation of forests, the pollution of rivers, the deterioration of craft standards, and the general degradation of existence including housing and arts, as well as the innumerable forms of public and private life that do not affect profits."[40] Given the current global crises driven by expanding and unregulated markets, the widespread revival of interest in Polanyi's warnings is no surprise.

In his recent film *La tierra y la sombra (Land and Shade)*, Colombian filmmaker César Augusto Acevedo presents a searing vision of the lived realities of capitalism's violence. It is a view from a delimited and local vantage point, with the global context implied indirectly. The film is set in the western Valle de Cauca, until recently a heavily forested region where an Afro-Colombian population lived on small farms, supporting themselves with traditional agriculture, based on rotation of local crops. Through the life of a single family, Acevedo shows us the ruins of this long-enduring traditional world through deforestation and the deathly onset of large-scale monoculture, which quickly followed the initial peace accords with FARC rebel forces in 2012. The film's physical landscape is dominated by the monotonous rows of sugar cane planted for conversion to ethanol. A single large tree stands outside the family's small house as a stark remnant of the lush forests that were leveled by the biofuel companies. The protagonist, Alfonso, has returned home after years of estrangement from his family. His adult son is bedridden, ill from the combined effects of smoke inhalation from the regular burning of the sugar cane and the constant use of herbicides. With their farm gone, his daughter-in-law works as a daily wage laborer in the fields alongside other dispossessed farmers, and they are often not paid. Alfonso tries to befriend his grandson by demonstrating the bird calls he learned as a child, but no bird ever responds to his efforts or is even seen. The land has become toxic, no longer a habitat for the flourishing of life. Acevedo's film, with quiet lucidity, traces the lines between the despoiled physical environment and the precariousness of social existence that Rosa Luxemburg had described. Foregrounded in *Land and Shade* are the wounded individuals from whom the ability to thrive and to care for others has been stolen.

A scorched earth is the stifling of hope, the canceling of the possibility that the world could be restored or healed. This crushing of belief in renewal is perpetuated through the capturing and disempowering of youth. The assault on the young, which begins earlier and earlier in childhood, is a continuation of the neo-conservative backlash to the rebellions of the 1960s and the whole political counterculture of those years. Since the mid-1990s, the internet complex has been the overarching means for not just neutralizing the insurgent energies of youth but for preventing youth from experiencing and knowing itself. To ward off any developments resembling the youth movements of the 1960s, it became essential to deny youth the spaces and times for even limited autonomy and collective self-recognition. Over the past two decades, young people have been deflected from political agency and have become the sector onto which demands for technological conformity and consumption have been most unsparing. Notable are the ceaseless efforts to cultivate habits and predictable behaviors to last a lifetime. Untold millions are spent researching "the neural foundations of preference formation." Generational segments (Gen Xers, Gen Zs, etc.) are invented by a pseudo-sociology to define the homogeneous consumerist tasks that are intended as an inescapable mass destiny. However, in broad areas of impoverishment in the Global South and elsewhere, the young are subjected to different and more ruthless forms of deprivation brought on by austerity, indebtedness, famine, and state terror.

In question is not a programmed acceleration into adulthood but, rather, the envelopment of most waking time by computers in the classroom, social media on phones, gaming, and other streams of content. Of course, there has been extensive discussion and debate about young people and digital technologies, but what is rarely stated is that they are being dispossessed of their youth. They are being denied the possibility of the exhilarating discovery of one's own uniqueness and the stirrings of self-love as the basis for initiation into the world through friendships, sexuality, and creativity. The vulnerable sensory world of the children and adolescents who inhabit the internet complex is now overwhelmingly one of addictive stimulation and electro-luminescent homogeneity. Most are condemned to dysfunctional and deteriorating schools which are increasingly modelled on prisons.[41] Ever more frequent school shootings become an additional burden of anxiety, fear and neglect. Young people are prompted to find their own thoughts boring or worthless and corporate platforms train them to exchange or display the most superficial features of who they are. Spontaneity vanishes amid incessant images of violence, joyless pornography, cruelty and mockery. Music, in spite of its global commodification, remains one of the few ways they can contrive "a bare minimum of singularity."[42] But, overall, there is a production of subjects who are denied the ability to build a reservoir of memory and experience. The continual adjusting to the shifting fashions and signifiers of social media recalls Hannah Arendt's warning that "clichés, stock phrases, standardized codes of expression and conduct have the socially recognized function of protecting us against reality, that is, against a claim on our thinking."[43]

Young people are shut off from the sensuous experience of wonderment, which the philosopher Hans Jonas describes as "seeing the world for the first time with new eyes," making possible the birth of conscience and empathy.[44] Wonderment now is numbed or displaced by whatever is promoted as technologically "awesome." Online life generates needs that are manageable within its self-sufficient enclosure, and it regulates what is permissible to dream. It is only when desires and hopes cling to life in a shared physical world, no matter how broken, that a person grows capable of refusal, and can feel enmity toward the powers and institutions that assault and smother those hopes. There's an episode in Shirley Clarke's 1963 film, *The Cool World*, involving the teenage prostitute LuAnne, who leads a degraded existence servicing members of a Harlem street gang. One winter weekend she goes with the gang leader, Duke, who is also her pimp, to visit a deserted Coney Island where she sees the ocean for the first time. Quite simply, her unexpected encounter with the cold, gray expanse of a limitless sky and sea sparks a momentary, inchoate flash of self-recognition, emboldening her so that, when briefly unattended, she disappears.

One of the core elements of New Left politics in the 1960s was the assumption that young people, regardless of their relation to labor or production, were oppressed and estranged by the values and demands of twentieth-century capitalist society. A widely shared belief that the young were uniquely resistant to technocratic and institutional integration found expression in the writings of Paul Goodman, Theodore Roszak, Raoul Vaneigem and many others. Of course, "youth" has been historically shaped in many different ways, but one relatively constant feature has been the idea of a transitional or liminal phase shaped by ritual or cultural practices in order to accomodate assimilation into the adult world. However, by the mid-twentieth century, in much of the West, various mechanisms and inducements of integration had ceased to function successfully, allowing new openings for experimentation and the exploration of alternative pathways and rebellions. Although decades have passed, the persistence of corporate media derision and caricature of 1960s counterculture barely conceals the persistent trepidation at even the partial refusal of prohibitions and mandates on the part of such large numbers. The goal now is to disallow youth from ever having the circumstances in which to imagine and build a future that belongs to them. Instead, there is endless news about young people "creatively" and "disruptively" making use of their digital tools and platforms. The priority is to derail the possibility of a potentially rebellious youth, and, in order to conceal their jobless, worldless future, there is the dismal fiction of a generation aspiring to become "influencers," founders of start-ups, or otherwise aligned with spiritless entrepreneurial values.

But the young are not the only ones dispossessed of times and spaces for interhuman connection. The neutralizing of non-financializable forms of social interaction injures the communicative capacities of all human beings. This is accomplished not only through the relentless lying and disinformation which have long been part of the conduct of states and powerful institutions. More important now are the deranging effects of the maelstrom of debilitating incoherence in which we are now permanently submerged. The internet is the digital counterpart of the vast, rapidly expanding garbage patch in the Pacific Ocean. Within it, the accumulating detritus of global networks choke off any clearing in which living exchanges between individuals or communities can occur. The immense and unending agglomeration of data, whether as images or language, produces a numbing cacophony and disorientation in which thinking is constricted and the possibility of dialogue crowded out. For millions of people every day, the primary interaction with others is the soon-to-be-forgotten mention of some floating particles of this online morass. One of the foremost achievements of the so-called knowledge economy is the mass production of ignorance, stupidity, and hatefulness.

The philosopher Jürgen Habermas argued at length that language, as a medium of mutual understanding, is not just an important component of the lifeworld but is constitutive of it. Much of his work analyzed the processes through which the lifeworld was subjected to the instrumentalizing forces of capitalist economy, media, and technoscience. However, even in the face of what he saw as "the colonization of the lifeworld," Habermas was ever hopeful that new forms of media might help support public spheres in which consensus-based communication could occur between "responsible actors." Writing around 1980, Habermas's optimism about an enlightened modernity grounded in "communicative action" was tempered by his observation that the lifeworld would be as good as extinguished if communication became subject to coordinated and constant forms of deception and distortion.[45] Now, forty years later, an outcome he considered unlikely is close to being realized, and our everyday praxis is sabotaged unremittingly by programmed unintelligibility and duplicity.

Since the 1970s a number of theorists, notably Henri Lefebvre, have shown how capital transforms familiar social environments into "abstract space," that is, into milieus compatible with the forms of exchange and circulation on which global markets depend. For Lefebvre, this was the reduction of the world "to a 'plan' existing in a void and endowed with no other qualities." It is the making of a *tabula rasa*, vacated of whatever is unique or resistant to being made exchangeable. Lefebvre specifies that abstract space is not literally homogeneous; rather, "it simply has homogeneity as its goal."[46] In his account of these fundamental tendencies of capital, some mistook "abstract" for a technologically generated order or regularity. Now, decades later, we have a better view of the scorched-earth realities of the *tabula rasa* to which we are headed: a ravaged and plundered earth, with more regions made uninhabitable and unrestorable. Political theorist Andreas Malm has supplemented Lefebvre's model in crucial ways. Malm shows that for all the demonstrably abstract features which allow the untrammeled mobility of capital, abstract space depends intrinsically on terrestrial resources, in particular fossil fuels. The mobility of capital is paradoxically made possible by *immobile* strata of concentrated energy. "The enhanced freedom to locate and relocate, refine and manufacture, order and dispatch, import and export is guaranteed by mines, wells, gas fields: large concentrates of techno-mass inseparable from the ground below."[47] Equally important are the massive and wide-ranging forms of violence needed both for the imposition of this abstract space and for the capture and control of terrestrial energy stocks. In this sense, capitalism necessitates the elimination of whatever might impede or obstruct the physical or immaterial flows intrinsic to capital accumulation through demolition, clear-cutting, mountain-top leveling, mining, hydraulic fracturing, and the murder of civilian populations to secure resource-rich territory.

Long before capitalism, Roman conquest brought with it the installation of abstract plans for encampments and towns. These geometrical layouts were physical and cognitive extensions of the Roman core to the periphery and they functioned as repeatable templates of imperial control. Robert Pogue Harrison has discussed how the great temperate forests of northern Europe were both a physical obstacle to Roman expansion and a phenomenon that disrupted perceptual and spatial mastery.[48] The vast woodlands confounded observers who sought visual certainties and regularities for the mapping and domestication of conquered lands. Instead, the forest with its vagaries of light, shadow, uncertain distances, and the impenetrable abundance of living matter was an environment that would only be dominated by eliminating it. Many centuries later, also motivated by imperial ambitions, the American military were confronted by the impenetrability of the Vietnamese forests and the concealment they provided for insurgents. The horrifying use of defoliants and herbicides, including Agent Orange, continued for over ten years, not just to create the visibility needed for aerial targeting but also as a genocidal strategy of destroying crops to deny food to the population.

The most consequential event in recent history resulting in a provisional abstract space was World War II. Long encumbered with ideological myths and historical fabrications, it's important to understand how this war, for the victors, was an operation of modernization achieved through unparalleled devastation. For global capitalism, it accomplished the essential dissolution of obsolete borders, languages, forms of sovereignty and finance or anything else that impeded the remaking of the planet for domination by mega-cartels and a permanent warfare state. It was the final clearing away of the residual shards of a premodern Europe. The savagery of the bombings of Hiroshima and Nagasaki and the fire bombings of Dresden, Hamburg, and Tokyo, all without military necessity, were demonstrations of the irrelevance and disposability of a lifeworld and its inhabitants according to the imperatives that were to shape the post-war Pax Americana. As many have shown, the war and its immediate aftermath gave birth to the National Security State, abetted by the emerging nexus of chemical, aerospace, and microelectronics industries. The famed ENIAC computer was completed in 1946 and immediately used by the US military for calculations to predict trajectories of artillery or rockets; in the same year, it played a decisive role in the development of the first hydrogen bomb. Even in the years immediately after the war, some wanted to use atomic weapons to guarantee the unchallenged permanence of the new order. One of the most celebrated twentieth-century mathematicians, John von Neumann, advocated (unsuccessfully) for a massive pre-emptive nuclear strike on all the major cities and industrial centers of the Soviet Union.[49] Chemical cartels began the industrialization of agriculture with pesticides and herbicides alongside the continuing development of chemical weapons for use on civilian populations. Life, whether of the body, of ecological rhythms, or of social resilience became not just an object to be controlled and exploited but to be made into a potential object of extermination.

Although discounted and trivialized, it remains revelatory that the internet complex is, in part, a product of the Cold War institutions in which scientists and technocrats routinely planned for outcomes involving mass annihilation. As is well known, ARPANET was designed in the 1960s as a "distributed" command and control network, intended to survive an all-out nuclear attack. Even if much of the network was destroyed along with most life on the planet, it would continue to be operational because of built-in redundancy of pathways and the absence of centralized switches. The goal was "to maintain survivable control of US nuclear forces" so that the network would retain the retaliatory capacity to launch whatever missiles remained intact. Thus, in question is a system whose functionality is not only divorced from any human context but expressly designed for circumstances when society and its members no longer meaningfully exist. In spite of the half century that has elapsed since ARPANET, and in spite of all the apparatuses appended to it, it's impossible to exorcise the terror of the mass relocation of social life to a network architecture originally conceived for the final abstract space, for the terminal *tabula rasa*. The uprooting and herding of populations all over the world onto the internet is confirmation of Paul Virilio's insistence, which seemed hyperbolic in the 1980s, that what used to be civilians are now permanently targeted elements in a new logistics of war adapted to the speeds of data networks. This was part of Virilio's larger argument that the ever-expanding war-making machine cannot coexist with civil society and that a foundation of the military's agenda is "societal non-development."[50]

The philosopher Simone Weil, writing in 1943 several months before her death, identified a spiritual crisis of "uprootedness" as one of the most injurious consequences of world war and the dominance of a money economy. Her account has nothing in common with reactionary appeals to land and soil; for her, to be uprooted was to be denied "real, active and natural participation in the life of a community."[51] She emphasized that one can remain geographically stationary and yet become torn away from a shared connection to the past or mutually nurtured expectations for the future. No matter one's environment, whether urban or rural, Weil elaborated on the necessity of having multiple roots in it, roots that engage one practically through work and morally through attentiveness to others. In our present moment, all the new forms of digital uprootedness support the illusion of autonomy, while any vague longings for enduring emotional connections are thwarted by the transience and homogeneity of online interactions. Inevitably, this reinforces our uncomprehending indifference to the unraveling of the lifeworld around us. We become blind to the mounting uprootings of a different kind, merciless and terrifying, which are on course to shatter our techno-complacency. Famine, drought, and warfare continue to force millions from their homes and once-functioning communities, leaving behind lands and whole regions that can no longer support life. By casting our lot in with the "becoming digital" of everything, we drift in the hallucination that it will all somehow persist. In spite of our hopes and intentions, we unthinkingly perpetuate the disaster of the global present and doom ourselves to inherit the terminal *tabula rasa* of scorched earth capitalism.

2

Technological truths already attained can only become practicable under the social relations of communism.

Karl Marx, 1851

With daily news of massive loss of Arctic sea ice, melting of glaciers in Greenland and Antarctica, and fires burning across the Siberian permafrost, it may seem irrelevant to note a more insignificant feature of the earth's vanishing cryosphere. Located on the edge of Yosemite National Park in the Sierra Nevada mountains is the Lyell Glacier, or what little is left of it. For many years, it was among the most visited of the several hundred glaciers once present in the contiguous forty-eight states, but, in 2010, it was declared effectively dead. Now, it consists of scattered patches of dwindling ice, darkened by atmospheric soot. Here is not only the wreckage of a glacier, but the ruin of once influential, even unassailable assumptions about time, permanence, or what is "here to stay."

The glacier was assigned its Euro-American name in the 1850s, following the violent expropriation of the Yosemite Valley from its indigenous inhabitants. For educated elites, whether in Europe or North America, the conjunction of the words "Lyell" and "glacier" was a harmonious fit. By the middle of the nineteenth century, the Scottish geologist Charles Lyell was widely known for his claim that significant geological changes occurred only over immense spans of time. Tremendous transformations of the earth had taken place, but slowly and imperceptibly, through processes of erosion and sedimentation taking far longer than the brief frame of recorded history. One illustration of Lyell's "gradualism" were glaciers which, from the human point of view, seemed like eternal presences despite their imperceptibly slow movement. Lyell acknowledged the periodic occurrence of violent and anomalous events such as volcanic eruptions and earth-quakes, but believed they had little impact on the constancy of long-term processes.

The work of James Hutton in the 1790s had introduced the influential notion of "deep time," posing a temporal scale of the earth's history so vast as to be sublimely incommensurable with human experience. Building on Hutton's work, Lyell dramatized the inconceivable slowness with which the state of the earth is modified from our perspective, even as he showed how the earth never ceases being "the theater of reiterated change, of slow but never-ending fluctuations."[1] An intellectual and cultural frame-work emerged that positioned the terrestrial environment as passive and impervious to human intervention. In Lyell's words, "the aggregate force exerted by man is truly insignificant" and nature was "no longer a significant actor from the standpoint of human history and social science."[2] Economic modernization required the earth and its structures to become distanced and objectified, like a landscape painting, to contemplate and study, but at the same time its seemingly infinite reserve of resources had to remain directly accessible for exploitation and the acquisition of wealth. Lyell did speculate that the earth's atmosphere might grow warmer over tens of thousands of years into the future, but recent developments, such as the disappearance of gigantic polar ice sheets within a human lifespan, would have been unimaginable for him.

Now, with ever upward revisions of climate warming rates, it becomes difficult to assume that anything is "here to stay," except radioactive waste, micro-plastics, and "forever" chemicals. We are living amid the mounting consequences of believing human actions to be independent of the world of which we are a part. But, as long as we conceive of our task as the staving off of an *impending* planetary catastrophe, we fail to understand, as Walter Benjamin and many others have said, that the real catastrophe is the perpetuation of the way things are and have been, of all the forms of imperial violence, economic injustice, racial and sexual terror, and ecological ravagement. It's a moment when the continuities and habituations of the present need to be disrupted and when gradualism in political praxis is no longer an option. At this unique historical crossroads, the evocation of catastrophe is increasingly appropriated as a weapon of corporate and military power and their techno-modernist mouthpieces. Often, the same authorities who insist on the permanence of the global institutions and 24/7 networks of the digital age are also the ones posing global warming as a crisis so huge that the only solution is carbon-capture geo-engineering, requiring efforts on a scale much greater than the Manhattan project. Together, these contradictory messages are a double bind that breeds paralysis and fatalism. In either of these scenarios (perpetual present of low-wage work, endless new devices, and mini-series binge-watching, or military/corporate management of planetary disaster), the future is presented as the maintenance of existing power relations—projections from which egalitarian forms of post-capitalism or eco-socialism are excluded.

Despite such posturing, there are now far fewer grandiose characterizations of capitalism as indestructible, as a vampiric system periodically killed off only to rise again in some new guise. The cliché of capitalism's perpetual renewability is itself exhausted. With any luck we've heard the last of the maxim once tirelessly repeated by academic postmodernists and others, that it's easier to imagine the end of the world than the end of capitalism. During the heyday of this sentiment, there were millions in the Global South and elsewhere whose political imaginations were not so narrowly paralyzed. Several analyses in the wake of the crisis of 2008 argue that the game is nearly over: capitalism has no more cards to play, and there has been an inexorable erosion of value production. For example, the late Robert Kurz maintained that the much-vaunted shift, beginning in the 1970s, to an information economy led by service industries never came close to matching its hyperbolic characterizations and failed to inaugurate a new phase of accumulation.[3] For Kurz, the 2008 collapse was inseparable from the dominance of micro-electronics and computing in the global economy. Capitalism, he showed, is fatally weakened when work and the time of work cease to be the main source and measure of wealth. As one of his interviewers summarized: "Here begins the extermination of the golden egg hen of capitalism, labor."[4] Capitalism approaches its exhaustion when human productivity is not just augmented by technology but *replaced* by it.

For Wolfgang Streeck, capitalism is in an advanced stage of disintegration and will eventually come apart "under the weight of the daily disasters produced by a social order in profound, anomic disarray."[5] He sees a terminal condition of entropic disorder in which society ceases to have stable institutions capable "of protecting individuals from accidents and monstrosities of all sorts." Others emphasize external limits as markers of the inevitable collapse. Several years ago, David Graeber observed that "capitalism as an engine of infinite expansion and accumulation cannot, by definition, continue in a finite world. Now that India and China are buying in as full players, it seems reasonable to assume that within forty years at most, the system will hit its physical limits. Whatever we end up with at that point, it will not be a system of infinite expansion. It will not be capitalism; it will be something else. However, there is no guarantee that this something will be better. It might be considerably worse."[6]

As the impossibility of continued growth and accumulation becomes more obvious every month, many of the imaginaries of "progress" that accompanied the various metamorphoses of capitalism have faded away. For nearly 200 years, these had sustained delusional expectations that material and scientific advancements were moving toward a future prosperity in which everyone would share.[7] Now, one marker of terminal capitalism is the absence of any substantive or credible promises of a better future. Some have argued that as of the 1990s, a new kind of historical awareness, often labeled "presentism," has begun to displace the various "futurisms" of the preceding two centuries.[8] Elements of presentism include all the technological innovations designed to abolish time or function in "real time," which privilege the "now" and foster the illusion of instantaneity and immediate availability. That every service or product should be accessible "on demand" presupposes a reality unmoored from spatial, material, or temporal constraints. A related feature is the use of computing for risk analyses, forecasts, and simulations, seeking to identify multiple outcomes and to minimize uncertainty; in a sense, to occupy and neutralize the future before it occurs.

For the dominant global powers, the only tolerable horizon of expectation is one that confirms and extends the imperatives of the present, in which the unforeseen and unpredictable have been minimized or eliminated. But it's possible to argue that "presentism" is nothing new, and indeed can be affiliated with the many ways capitalism has shaped the experience of temporality. The French-Hungarian sociologist Joseph Gabel, in the 1960s, described how capitalism depends on a negation of historical time and a positing of "progress" as a quantitative succession of present moments that maintains existing social and economic arrangements. "The privileged system is considered as perfect and extra-temporal," and therefore as immune to radical or qualitative transformation. In a reified, technocratic society, Gabel wrote, "history can never be understood as the expression of creativity and spontaneity. Consequently, the undeniable fact of change forces itself on this consciousness of immediacy as a catastrophe."[9]

Part of our current crisis is the indifferent acceptance of the now banalized notion that our future is being invented by a small number of powerful corporations. Decisions about what product lines will sustain profits and growth have effectively made these companies into the official futurologists of our time, the regulators of our expectations. According to Webster's Dictionary, the first uses of the words "futurology" and "futurologist" occurred in 1946. It is not coincidental that this specialization came into play at the end of the war, amid a broken world to be overseen and reshaped by American military and economic superiority. To forestall or nullify divergent hopes for a future of disarmament and international cooperation, a pseudo-science emerged whose task was to define the contours of a near future that conformed to the needs and requirements of American corporations and their imperial ambitions. Although some of the fictions and exclusions of futurology go well back into the nineteenth century, 1946 is when the dominant articulations of collective expectations become restricted to official experts, think tanks, economic forecasters and best-selling gurus. Of course, technocratic depictions of the future concocted by elites are hardly new, but for over a century, from Henri de Saint-Simon in the 1820s to Walther Rathenau after World War I, advocates of economic and social rationalization almost always imagined less oppressive forms of labor and mitigations of social inequality in their forward-looking visions. In the 1920s, H. G. Wells portrayed a future that included a democratic world federation, disarmament, universal education, and even some limits on private enterprise.[10]

However, the take-off of post-war consumer society required a decisive delinking of the future from any imagination of transformed social relations. The future became inseparable from carefully tended projections of scientific and technological progress coinciding with a range of new tasks for post-war consumers, but in which existing political and economic hierarchies would remain fixed in place. In part, the arrival of the Atomic Age with its new forms of global terror and mass death had to be repackaged and domesticated into promises of increasing abundance and leisure, enabled by "clean" nuclear energy, automation, blinking IBM mainframes and a host of other alleged advances. In the work of another science-fiction writer, one sees how much had changed since Wells wrote in 1920. Arthur C. Clarke, by the late 1950s, was an early incarnation of the public "futurologist," with his bestselling non-fiction book *Profiles of the Future*. Written between 1958 and 1961, much of it originally published in *Playboy* magazine, the book can stand for hundreds of parallel accounts in which the future is presented as a catalog of disconnected scientific, medical, or technological innovations but which tacitly confirm the immutability of the existing social order. For conservative sci-fi writers and futurists like Clarke, the sources of radical change can only be quasi-theological events like the arrival of super-intelligent aliens or the evolution of human beings into a disembodied overmind.

By the late 1970s, most of the sensational features of Clarke's futurology and that of many of his contemporaries circa 1960 (such as colonies on Mars, speed-of-light travel, teleportation, or dolphins speaking English) gave way to less exciting prognostication that was little more than rhetorically inflated economic forecasting. Whether the book was called *Future Shock* (1970) or *Megatrends* (1982), the future soon became about "outcomes," or, more bluntly, the winners and losers in a post-industrial or information-based economy. The buzzwords then were decentralization, networks, non-linear systems, and globalization; but behind the verbiage lay the anti-utopian forecast of a world in which everything was determined by the desultory metamorphoses of the free market. In the past decade there has been a huge increase in such speculation on the near future, but almost exclusively in terms of specific technological innovations and their consequences for institutions and investors. The title of a recent book encapsulates the claustrophobic frame of futurology: *The Two-Second Advantage: How We Succeed by Anticipating the Future*.

Of course, there were momentous challenges to the official futurist pronouncements, especially during the global upheavals of the 1960s and early 1970s. Equally significant were the events of 1989–91, although the suddenness with which they unfolded had different consequences. Now we can look back at the implosion of the Soviet Union as the onset of some of the influential "here to stay" narratives: the end of history and the arrival of a unipolar planet of market democracies. It's easy to forget the contested stakes of those developments. The end of the Soviet Union and its hold over Eastern Europe occurred so unexpectedly that it opened a popular imagination to the idea that a seemingly unassailable facade of political power might in fact conceal a flimsy house of cards. For leaders in the US and Western Europe, despite their gloating, this was nonetheless a dangerous exhibition in need of countervailing measures. The early 1990s were also a brief window when the end of the of the Cold War seemed surely to bring with it the promise of a "peace dividend." Everywhere, there were expectations that some of the massive resources expended on war-making would be redirected elsewhere. It was as if a weight had been lifted off a collective social consciousness, igniting the revivifying hope that another kind of world was possible. A wounded capacity for utopian thought and praxis was, momentarily at least, brought back to life.

For the managers of the new hegemon in the West, expectations of actual "peace dividends," in whatever form, had to be quickly nullified or diverted. Thus, anticipations of a more egalitarian, non-militarized society were displaced by a future conforming to neoliberal priorities. The availability of the World Wide Web in the early 1990s, framed by absurd claims about cyberspace and virtual reality, was pivotal in this operation of tranquilization. Alongside the celebration of globalization, the internet was hailed as the portal to a new age of connectedness and opportunity. And to ensure that the "peace dividend" was forgotten, the 1990s were marked by a new sequence of high-tech wars with calamitous US military interventions in Kuwait, Iraq, Somalia, and Kosovo/Serbia.

For those in the East, the apparent opportunity to build a socialist society free of bureaucratic authoritarianism was exhilarating, especially in the German Democratic Republic, but it was rapidly quashed. The brutality and callousness with which capitalist values were imposed in Russia, seemingly overnight, is recounted by numerous voices in Svetlana Alexievich's oral history *Secondhand Time*:

> They turned Russia into a Western junkyard full of worn-out rags and expired medicines . . . The Soviet regime? It wasn't ideal but it was better than what we have today. No one was excessively rich or poor, there were no beggars or abandoned children. Old people could live on their pensions, they didn't have to collect bottles and food scraps off the street . . . my "horrible Soviet upbringing" taught me to think about people other than myself.[11]

Now, three decades later, the products, systems, and services which media and technology companies trumpet as forthcoming are confirmations of a vanished future. We are constantly updated about what we must buy and when it must be replaced as it slips into uselessness, and, implicitly, we are cautioned that to hope for anything beyond these cycles of consumption is pointless. With capitalism entering its terminal phase, on a planet disfigured by neoliberal austerity and environmental collapse, there is no longer even the pretense that scientific and technical development is aligned with human purposiveness or needs. The once fashionable but nonsensical predictions of a coevolution in which humans and machines would gradually merge into hybrid entities have been abandoned by all but a few psychotic "singularity" cultists. As this book went to press, some of the most heavily publicized areas of techno-innovation included AI, robotics, neurosciences, augmented/virtual reality, autonomous vehicles, nanotechnology, genomics, and the Internet of Things (IoT). Each of these topics could be considered individually, but together they convey a sense of the suffocating occupation of a world from which human agency and creativity has been deleted. The ongoing promotion of AI, robotics, and the IoT is a forlorn announcement of the relegation of humans, as working and living beings, to the periphery of technological systems, and also, for many, into debt, hunger, illness, and impoverishment. The philosopher Günther Anders, writing in the 1950s, outlined how the telos of modern technological culture was the installation of "a world without us." He did not mean the disappearance of people but rather the encroachment of autonomous systems that render obsolete any decision-making based on the needs of human communities. What distinguishes Anders's position from related critiques is his insistence that nuclear weapons, since their use in World War II, have become the paradigmatic technological object: for their absolute efficiency, for their perpetual disclosure of the irrelevance and disposability of living beings, and for their utter remoteness from any claims on behalf of a human and natural world.[12]

The advent of 5G networks signals this irrelevance in the overwhelming preponderance of data flows between "things" rather than communication between people. That billions of machines are "*communicating* with each other" indicates the current emptiness of this verb and the degradation of its rich social etymology. The new speeds of streaming computing power between different devices and networks allow sensor-equipped "things" to perform actions autonomously, and the digital services used by people will be ceaselessly adjusting and updating their operations as feedback on behaviors is processed. Such high computational speeds render hopelessly obsolete the time needed for reflective deliberation between human beings. We are getting closer to an actualization of the cybernetic paradigm described by the Tiqqun collective as

> a radically new structuring of the subject, whether individual or collective. The aim is to hollow it out. It is no longer a matter of separating the subject from traditional exterior ties as the liberal hypothesis has demanded, but of depriving the subject of all substance. Each person was to become a fleshless envelope, the locus of an infinite feedback loop.[13]

These innovations are usually presented to the public as the convenience of living and working in "smart" environments where "everything is done for you before you've even thought of it." This is exactly what is at stake: the dispossession of thought, and the evaporation of what used to be understood as interiority and volition. Whether the AI-driven robotic Internet of Things is ever even partially realized is less important now than how its disclosure of human expendability contributes to demoralization and the crushing of hope. One awaits this future as one would await death.

Luis Suarez-Villa has outlined how twenty-first-century corporations are transforming the whole of society into a vast experimental laboratory to drive the agenda of technocapitalism, namely, "to conquer and colonize most every aspect of human existence (and nature itself)."[14] He sees one of the current goals of corporate power as the management of mass consumption habits and the production of compliant individuals who conform to the priorities of corporate power. New advances in biopharmacology and neuromarketing are just some of the outcomes of this expanded field of experimentalism. If this sounds exaggerated, consider these words from the website of the billionaires' World Economic Forum: "The Fourth Industrial Revolution is the first where the tools of technology can become literally embedded within us and even purposefully change who we are at the level of our genetic makeup. It is completely conceivable that forms of radical human improvement will be available within a generation."[15] This megalomaniacal goal of integrating human biology with information technology is unlikely to proceed very far, but it's nonetheless revealing of the deranged ambitions propelling current corporate agendas. Philosopher Federico Campagna has described what is at stake in the radical disparity between living beings and increasingly powerful information networks: "The record-shattering investments in Big-Data systems and technology rest on the belief that there can't possibly be anything ontologically relevant that couldn't, at least potentially, be reduced to the serial units of the language of data." A living person who refuses or is incapable of this reduction, he writes, "is instantly stripped of any legitimate claim to presence in the world."[16]

The new capabilities of AI and quantum computing are being developed for the sectors that benefit most from their deployment: banking and finance, security and intelligence agencies, and the military. All these operate in data-rich environments and the processing power and speed with which risk analysis and automated decision-making can occur is essential to their success and global dominance. The installation of 5G networks is especially critical for the military's ambition of maintaining "full spectrum dominance" by linking all of its land, sea, air, and satellite assets into a single inter-communicating assemblage. Anders's postulation of technologies that dispense with human beings is realized in the creation of great wealth without labor, in a military that plans electronic wars without soldiers and in social media where bots far outnumber actual people. These tools are dependent on the plunder and theft of social wealth and natural resources, preventing them from ever being in the service of anything resembling a common good (other than the downloading of hours of video content in a millisecond). The expanded parameters of machine "intelligence" driving global finance and the autonomous war-making platforms of the military make a mockery of the pious claims that AI will benefit human needs. "Big data" and AI will only intensify existing global inequalities and expedite the development of new weapons systems.

There are some who worry that the touted capabilities of AI, 5G networks and the Internet of Things will coalesce into a smoothly functioning panoptic arrangement of social control, but this is never going to happen. The reality will be a patchwork of competing and incompatible systems and components, resulting in defectiveness, breakdowns, and inefficiencies. The capitalist logic of continual disruption through planned obsolescence, ever greater technical complexity, cost-cutting and the rushed introduction of unneeded upgrades conflicts with the stability needed for the efficient functioning of authoritarian control. Fearful anticipations of a totalizing future of digital surveillance and regulation are not only exaggerated but are an impediment to realizing how free we are, in fact, to refuse the mandates of empire and adopt alternate ways of living.

According to the technocratic futurists of the mid-twentieth century, we should by now be thriving in gleaming, poverty-free cities connected by high-speed rail, surrounded by material abundance from automated factories, and taking vacations on Mars. Instead we are living amid decay and fatal disrepair: jetliners crashing because of cutbacks on safety features, water systems poisoned, failing power grids, petrochemical plants exploding, sea level rise threatening nuclear reactors and much else. There are growing mountains of discarded and unrecyclable solar panels and wind turbines, pedestrians killed by driverless vehicles because they behaved "illogically," and the collapse of shoddily built edifices like the Ponte Morandi in Genoa or the Miami condominium, presaging the inevitable crumbling of millions of other concrete structures as their internal steel elements corrode. In the words of the artist Robert Smithson, "we are surrounded by evidence of a succession of man-made systems mired in abandoned hopes."[17] The internet complex, now compounded by the Internet of Things, struggles to conceal its fatal dependence on the rapidly deteriorating built world of industrial capitalism. Contrary to all the grand proposals, there never will be significant restoration or replacement of all the now broken infrastructure elements put in place during the twentieth century.

Any effective imagination of a post-capitalist material culture must confront the inseparability of modern technology from the institutional formations of modern science. We are currently overwhelmed from all sides by reverential exaltations of "science" and of the unimpeachable authority of "the scientists" who will deliver us from the climate crisis. The absurdity of this sanctification of one of the primary agents of biosphere destruction—including global warming—is evident to many, but there is a strict prohibition on openly acknowledging it. Science, in its many powerful institutional manifestations, is now essentialized as an a priori source of truth, existing above economic interests or social determinations and exempt from historical or ideological evaluation. It is the one remaining mirage of legitimacy behind which global capital continues its rampage of planetary looting and destruction. The marginal figures of the altruistic climatologist or oceanographer are foregrounded as camouflage for the structural complicity of most scientific research with corporate and military priorities. In the face of reactionary attacks on all forms of knowledge and learning, our response should not be a mindless celebration of a fairytale account of "science." Such cowardly obsequiousness is an anti-intellectualism as damaging as the right-wing embrace of ignorance. The voluminous and many-sided critique of the limits and failings of Western science has been rendered invisible and unmentionable. Contributors to this essential body of thought include some of the most discerning philosophers, scientists, feminists, activists, and social thinkers of the last hundred or more years. We're at a moment when the survival of life on our planet depends on reanimating this critique, and recovering an unequivocal awareness of how most of the foundational paradigms of Western science have brought us to our current disastrous, possibly terminal, situation.

Unlike many on the left, French theorist Jacques Camatte had no such illusions in the early 1970s when he identified science as both servant and divinity of capitalism. He understood that science had become fully configured to be "the study of mechanisms of adaptation which will assimilate human beings and nature into the structure of capitalism's productive activity."[18] The full colonization of research by the military and corporations following World War II consummated the disappearance of meaningful distinctions between science and technology. Jean-François Lyotard saw the unconstrained development of capitalist technoscience as the final negation of the emancipatory project of modernity and the extinguishing of any illusions about the beneficent role of human reason.[19] The scientific method had long since become dependent on technology for creating the artificial, deracinated objects on which the method could be deployed. Nature and human beings are reduced and homogenized into techno-scientific abstractions. Indeed, as early as the 1600s, Western science had become one of the most powerful discursive supports for racism, misogyny, and the geno-cidal colonial projects originating in Europe and then in North America.

Alfred North Whitehead detailed some of the historical con-ditions for the rise of technoscience: he noted that the very nature of what previously had been thought of as "science" changed fundamentally in the nineteenth century. Scientific research became meaningful or valuable primarily for its potential to generate some application, product, or practical technique. "The greatest invention of the nineteenth century," he wrote caustically, "was the invention of the method of invention." Science defined itself, not by principles but through results. It became "a store-house of ideas for utilization," which clearly meant commercial, profit-making applications.[20] Whitehead noted the late-nine-teenth-century emergence of the methods by which abstract knowledge could be connected with technology and with unend-ing sequences of innovations. He singled out Germany as the country where "the boundless possibilities of technological advance" were first realized. Whitehead, presenting these obser-vations in his 1925 Lowell Lectures at Harvard, was too genteel

to state the obvious: that "the method of invention" was inseparable from the rise of industrial capitalism and its voracious
requirements. The modern state-capitalist vocation of science
(which Whitehead, Max Weber, Helmuth Plessner, and others
had identified by the 1920s) has clearly brought us to the
edge of catastrophe with its ceaseless flood of "utilizations."[21]
Currently, the shrill glorification of "science" is a desperate
maneuver of obfuscation, to forestall a wider recognition of the
disastrous inseparability of Western science and capitalism while
promoting the delusion that "science" will save us from its own
calamitous accomplishments, notably the current unravelling of
the earth system.

To take one of innumerable examples, the torrent of synthetic
chemicals poisoning air, water, soil, oceans, and the bodies of
every higher organism is certainly one of the most enduring
"accomplishments" of capitalist technoscience. Scientists themselves, not just corporate executives, bear direct responsibility for
the terminal wounding of living systems by plastics, herbicides,
pesticides, and petrochemical fertilizers, as well as for the toxic
impact of the 120,000 compounds (increasing every month) that
saturate ourselves and the environment. These compounds have
been produced for no other purpose than the facilitating of
manufacturing and technical processes, including military applications, and for enhancing, in thousands of ways, the unnecessary
"conveniences" of daily life and commerce. The global industrial
complex is dependent on a continual stream of new products
and is structurally incapable of limiting or regulating itself in
any meaningful way. The actuality of a world made into a
terminal waste dump by technoscience is not an anomaly that
could have been, or might yet be, put right; it is intrinsic to the
operations of scorched earth capitalism. When one considers the

harmful innovations of synthetic biology, nanotechnology, social robotics, and autonomous weapons systems, to name just a few other areas, the knee-jerk veneration of "science" can only be understood as a capitulation to the ongoing assault on the life-world. For philosopher Jean-Pierre Dupuy, "anyone who believes that science and technology will manage to provide a solution to problems created by science and technology, does not believe in the reality of the future."[22]

A sign of the technoscientific curtailment of the future was Google's 2013 launch of a new division called Calico, the California Life Company. This research and development undertaking was formed, according to its promoters, "to explore the biology that controls lifespan" and to solve what it deemed to be the "problem" of aging. Although dozens of biotech and genomics firms are also pursuing and bringing to market anti-aging drugs and treatments, Google's entry into this sector was notable for different reasons and was greeted with predictable fanfare, for example, by *Time* magazine's cover with the company's trademark font posing the question "Can Google Solve Death?" The *Time* article cited a top executive who proclaimed that, building on all of Google's successes, "finally we're tackling aging," and said that lifespans of 500 years will be achievable. Whether or not Google ever brings any longevity products to market is irrelevant. It is significant as an open acknowledgment by a highly visible media corporation of the much broader neoliberal financialization of biological life, for Google is merely one participant in the ongoing reconceptualization of human life into a computational model for data processing and capital accumulation.

To suppress aging is to imagine life as a distended present, suspended from time and shielded from decay or change. For thousands of years, the finiteness of life has been what has given meaning, passion, and purpose to our existence, and to the ways we love and depend on others. To debase human finitude by proposing that individual longevity could become a sought-after biotech product for the affluent is part of the extinguishing of any values or beliefs that transcend the voraciousness of capitalism. The commodification and privatization of the future is now explicit, as "time to live" is assimilated into the logic of financial-ization. An anti-aging industry incites anxiety and fear—fear of frailty and dependence in a world in which most social forms of support have been weakened or eliminated. Even under minimal welfare state provisions, old age was a structural problem for cap-italism because of its relative unproductivity and diminished consumerism. Now, "aging" becomes part of the current pre-cariousness and disposability of all human life. For theorist Melinda Cooper, "neoliberalism is intent on profiting from the unregulated distribution of life chances."[23] At a time when organ-ized violence and social immiseration are overspreading every continent, Google's ambitions entail a harrowing neglect of the disparities that underpin the most urgent crises of subsistence and survival. Several billion people in the Global South have life expec-tancies that are two or three decades shorter than the eighty-plus years of many Western European nations, Japan, and elsewhere. In the slums of Mumbai, Lagos, and Rio, male life expectancy is less than forty years. From this perspective, aging is hardly a uni-versal or inevitable experience but rather a "lifestyle" problem of the affluent sectors of the planet. And now, in the US and elsewhere, "deaths of despair" among people in their thirties and forties are soaring, from drugs, alcohol, and suicide, all consequences of the daily pain of poverty, debt, loneliness, and depression.

As sociologist Zygmunt Bauman wrote, "Death is an emphatic denial of everything that the brave new world of modernity stood for."[24] This truth is especially unbearable for the global billionaire class. To them, consumed by delusions of omnipotence, the inevitability of death seems incomprehensible and absurdly unfair. The disparity between the brevity of an adult lifespan and the enormity of their wealth leads to unappeasable anger that money can't actually buy them time, endless time to exploit their fortunes and feed their narcissism. Hence the familiar pattern of the super-rich eagerly funding longevity research. In the 1920s, tycoons flocked to the clinic of Serge Voronoff for his monkey-gland "rejuvenation" therapy. By the 1970s, cryo-preservation was an option for some, who hoped that both their bodies and their assets could be frozen until resuscitation at some future time. Now, in Silicon Valley and elsewhere, billionaires are pursuing the transhumanist illusion that a mind can be uploaded to a computer, to attain some kind of biomechanical immortality. In the 1960s, Theodor Adorno profiled the techno-phile as a pathological manipulator: those who fetishize technology, he said, are "the cold ones" who have never known love, joy, or empathy. "This is not meant to be sentimental or moralistic but rather describes a deficient libidinal relation to other persons. These people are thoroughly cold; deep within themselves they must deny the possibility of love, must withdraw their love from other people before it can even unfold. And whatever of the ability to love somehow survives in them they must expend on devices."[25] Adorno noted that the dominant powers in "each epoch produces those personalities it needs societally."

As Norman O. Brown wrote in *Life Against Death*, "the inca-pacity to accept death results in the morbidity of an active death wish . . . death is overcome on condition that the real actuality of life pass into inert and dead things. A technological world is replete with forms of negative vitality. Nature and human nature come back in destructive forms."[26] This is an anticipatory vision, not just of billionaires seeking to live forever but also of our ongoing integration into systems like the Internet of Things. Admittedly, the life extension industry and its preposterous goal of commodifying quasi-immortality as a marketable product is a hyperbolic example. The figure of a mind uploaded into a computer is simply a metaphoric extension of a life lived within the stupefying parameters of the Internet of Things, within a head-mounted display, or through conversations with robotic voices—it is a life removed from immersion in living environments and cut off from the primary reciprocity between human beings, or between humans and animals and other species.

Brown's radical psychoanalytic account of the deathliness of a society dominated by technology anticipated what would become an influential current of 1960s counterculture: the refusal of devitalizing institutions and their repressive requirements. Artists, writers, and filmmakers portrayed the textures of fractured social worlds, and the emotional costs of inhabiting them. Thomas Pynchon's 1963 novel *V* explores the insinuation of the inanimate into individual and social experience, a process that began in the late nineteenth century. One of his characters voices a theme reiterated throughout the book: "A decadence is a falling away from what is human, and the further we fall the less human we become. Because we are less human, we foist off the humanity we have lost on inanimate objects and abstract theories." In William Burroughs's *Nova Express,* his "gods of Time-Money-Junk" prefigure today's Silicon Valley elites in their instrumentalizing of language and images into "a virus attack directed against affective animal life," a virus that enervates desire into patterns of addiction and automated habit. Philip K. Dick's novels of the mid-1960s, such as *Martian Time-Slip* and *Palmer Eldritch*, expose the human costs of "a peculiar malign abstractness" within a media- and commodity-saturated reality. Dick repeatedly details the schizophrenic depersonalization resulting from the collision of the self with spaces full of useless objects and with other people devoid of a capacity for empathy.

There were also imaginations of the world itself becoming literally inanimate, as indicated by the titles of Anna Kavan's *Ice* and J. G. Ballard's *The Crystal World*. Ballard explores some of the pathology of technophilia in his tale of European expats in an unnamed West African nation. Through some cosmic anomaly, an unstoppable process of crystallization has begun in the forest, transforming every living thing, including people, into beautiful but inert matter. Rather than a predictable narrative about heroic efforts to prevent this process from spreading over the planet, Ballard's novel follows the indolent attraction of his characters to this irresistible becoming-crystal and "the immunity from time" it seems to offer. Günther Anders, a decade earlier, had proposed that people were drawn to modes of "self-reification," hoping to "reduce or even abolish all other forms of human frailty and degradation."[27] These texts resonate with the well-known 1960s critiques of consumer capitalism and technocratic modernization. Together, they demonstrate that the social and psychic calamity of neoliberal globalization is hardly new, for it is, in many ways, an intensification of effects intrinsic to capitalism since the late nineteenth century. Max Weber's 1904 forecast of capitalism terminating in "mechanized petrification" is a reminder of what has long been evident to some.

Although the techno-modernists are motivated mainly by cynicism and opportunism, some are nostalgically attached to the long-gone chimera of an urban-based "machine age." Their regret is for the early to mid-twentieth-century era, when endless technological progress and urban growth seemed inevitable and when it might have been possible to believe in the messianic promises of a totally engineered world. One of the historical sources of techno-modernism and its illusions was the emergence in Europe of a new stratum of intelligentsia and administrators whose self-understanding included an identification with the expanding milieu of the metropolis. The countless images and portrayals of urban modernity then in circulation had, with few exceptions, a single element in common: the repudiation and erasure of agrarian life with all its rhythms, relationships, and forms of labor. Beginning in the 1850s, to be modern or to be cosmopolitan meant many things, but above all it required a sweeping disconnection from everything associated with the earthiness of rural existence, the smells and materialities of soil, manure, barnyard, animals, along with all the tactile immersion in the processes involved in the nurturing of organic life. There was also a related need to dissociate oneself from the limited horizons and ambitions of the landholding classes. More than just the expression of disdain or superiority in relation to peasants, farming, or the countryside, it was the onset of the technocratic dream of an artificial world organized around industrial production and rationalized decision-making.

The credibility of these illusions required covering up all the metabolic processes and flows at the heart of urban sociality. In this sense, the project of a standardized, instrumentalized megalopolis was driven by "a deep contempt for organic processes."[28] Thus, by the early twentieth century, the invocation of a machine age was dependent on the concealments effected by indoor plumbing, modernized sewers, relocation of animal slaughter, hospitalization of childbirth and the dying, and the advent of industrial agriculture. Whether Le Corbusier's "machine for living," Mies's Villa Tugendhat, or Hugh Hefner's gadget-filled bachelor penthouse, there were many sleek manifestations of the apparent autonomy of artificial environments, cut off from living systems. These coincided with the increasing marginalization of non-market spaces, uncompetitive commercial enterprises, and non-financializable activities.

The city/country disconnect was compounded, especially in England and France, by the dependence of urban centers on economic flows from the new "global countryside" of the dominated colonial periphery, where enslaved labor was rife. Impressionist painting confirmed the new urban mind-set by inventing an ornamental, suburbanized nature from which traces of agrarian labor were largely excluded. Baudelaire's mockery of efforts to preserve old-growth trees in Fontainebleau Forest, which he dismissed as "sanctified vegetables," or Mondrian's physical aversion to the disorderliness of nature are familiar, if superficial, illustrations of the modernist attachment to an exclusively urban universe. More importantly, Baudelaire understood early on the psychic costs of living in the emerging metropolis and, as critic Walter Benjamin understood, his "empathy with inorganic things was one of his sources of inspiration."[29] *Les Fleurs du Mal* gave lasting expression to what Manfredo Tafuri later called "the anguish of urban dynamism," referring to the modern economic and technological processes that operate with pitiless indifference to human hopes and values. Nonetheless, Baudelaire remained committed to his anti-nature stance and accepted the disjunctions and imperviousness of the city as inevitable and all-encompassing. The paradoxical map of the modern city was here disclosed: its inert and mineral surfaces made the city seem atemporal and imperishable, but any claim to monumental permanence was destabilized by the waste and destructiveness that accompany capitalist accumulation.

One of the most ruinous legacies of the attempts to segregate the city from the organic patterns and labor of subsistence are the nightmarish CAFOs (concentrated animal feeding operations) that cover large parts of rural America. These are a hidden facet of the modernist delusion that every aspect of pre-modern agrarian practices could be eliminated or reinvented as an industrial process. The CAFOs, and other forms of factory farming, are where billions of sentient animals, in horrific confinement and with their growth biochemically stimulated, are converted into food products. The waste, the non-stop slaughter, expanding manure lagoons, land and water poisoned, and air made unbreathable for underpaid workers are invisible and extraneous to everyone who relies on this system for subsistence. Modernity is inseparable from the systematic estrangement of human beings from subsistence and from the eradication of the habitats and ecosystems on which survival now depends.

In 1853, the year when Baron Haussmann began his remaking of the city of Paris, Rosa Bonheur's painting *The Horse Fair* was exhibited at the Salon. On the eve of an epochal transformation of urban space, the painting is shot through with some of the fractures and instabilities of that historical moment. This sixteen-foot-wide monumental image depicts a reciprocal and vital relation between city and countryside. It maps the centuries-old interdependencies of the rural milieus, where animals are raised, and the towns, through the phenomenon of the urban fair, the seasonal marketplace where trading, bartering and selling are conducted. Over the second half of the nineteenth century, there was a steady severing of both the symbolic and practical interconnections of city and country, especially as the de-linkage of wealth from land became one of the defining features of Western modernization. By 1871, the doomed insurgents of the Paris Commune, surrounded by hostile armies, became acutely aware of the broken ties between city workers and the peasantry beyond when there was no parallel rural uprising to support them. A related fate befell the Shanghai workers' militias in 1927.

By the early twentieth century, *The Horse Fair* and all Bonheur's work had become an object of cosmopolitan disparagement. More than other academic paintings, it was a special target of condescending male critics for whom it epitomized everything that was, for them, unfashionable or anti-modern. Even in recent years, there are visitors to New York's Metropolitan Museum who demonstrate their urbane sophistication by making clever, derisive remarks about *The Horse Fair* and its creator. But, once the painting is distanced from the now obsolete values of modernism, it can be engaged for what it is: an object infused with plural temporalities, with survivals and persistences that point to a future yet to be made. Despite its enthusiastic reception by bourgeois audiences in the 1850s, this was never a picture of a regressive ruralism. Molded by her utopian socialist upbringing, Bonheur made *The Horse Fair* into an image of the already contested spaces and identities of her present (and ours). It is emphatically a diagram of the city—the paving stones of the Boulevard de l'Hôpital, detailed in the foreground, are the surface on which the fair takes place, recalling the insurgent uses of such stones in barricades a few years earlier and posing their availability in times yet to come.

Bonheur's city is also marked by the presence of the Salpêtrière asylum, whose cupola with phallic clocktower is silhouetted against the sky. This place of confinement is a figure for the administered realm of binaries and assigned identities, for the regulation of madness and sanity, of gender, and, by extension, of the human and animal. Bonheur's own evasion of compulsory gender normativity carries over to her refusal of a clear boundary between her horses and their human handlers, one of whom is likely a self-portrait. The centripetal whirling of bodies, removed from a human–animal hierarchy, becomes an exuberant, carnival space/time of hybrid vitalities and intensities. It's a city yet to come, far removed from the masculinist necropolis of the machine age, in which animality would be repressed or excluded. Two decades later, Eadweard Muybridge's chronophotographs of horses, produced under the sponsorship of the railroad tycoon Leland Stanford, would be visual harbingers of the replacement of animal motive power by life-destroying forms of locomotion and combustion.

Now, in a time of terminal emergency, the painting intimates that the city of our damaged present has a future only if it is imagined as a field determined by our collaboration with other species, with non-human life, and with a post-capitalist rebuilding of biodiversity. The phantoms in Bonheur's multispecies image pose the necessity of urban ecosystems yet to come that will be "landscapes of entanglement, bodies with other bodies, times with other times."[30] The extraordinary 1994 rediscovery of the Chauvet cave in southern France, with its ageless paintings of animals, including horses, can be seen either as a random chance event or more usefully as the prophetic recovery, at a moment of extreme danger, of images from 30,000 years ago affirming a humanity that flourishes only through embracing its inseparability from the lifeworld of the animal and the non-human.

The revolutions of 1848, regardless of their outcomes, resulted from anticipations, nurtured over several decades, of a more egalitarian society based on worker self-management, forms of mutual aid and a rejection of private property. The emancipatory hopes raised by working-class struggles in 1848 coincided with the discovery of gold in California, an event widely publicized in Europe and which fostered a parallel and very different set of hopes around which happiness was imagined. Among the thousands who traveled to the gold fields seeking instant wealth were some of the defeated insurgents of the June uprisings and disillusioned participants in Fourierist and Icarian communities in North America.[31] As Ernst Bloch explained in *The Principle of Hope*, a human being "is a changeable and extensive complex of drives, a heap of changing and mostly badly ordered wishes." He also showed that drives themselves were historically shaped: "In the course of history, with its changing forms, hardly one kind of drive has remained the same. With new objects, different addictions and passions awake, of which no one had the slightest inkling yesterday. The acquisitive drive, which is itself only acquired anyway, has grown to an extent which was quite alien to pre-capitalist times."[32] Our contemporary billionaire culture has its roots in nineteenth-century images of easily amassed riches and the desires these aroused, relocating hope from anything based on shared responsibilities and mutuality to an individual craving for financial and symbolic capital.

It was amid the inequalities and class hierarchies of an expanding consumer society that popular dreams of wealth take on specifically modern contours, often provoked by the same underlying experiences of privation and humiliation. The perennial popularity of Dumas's *Count of Monte Cristo* (1844) derives from its compelling narrative of vast wealth enabling a belated righting of wrongs and the punishment of the agents of treachery and injustice, a formula that has been repeated many times. The

Dumas novel details how the recovery of a hidden treasure facilitates an elaborate scheme of revenge on the individuals who conspired to send the protagonist to life in prison. But, within the tale of vengeance, is the account of how an immense fortune allows Edmond Dantès, a sailor of modest means and education, to figuratively return from the dead and remodel himself into an omnipotent, aristocratic, multi-talented plutocrat. A key attraction of the novel is how unlimited affluence enables the self to be reinvented, to have plural identities, extraordinary means of mobility, influence, and sources of information. Its narrative parallels the historical transformation of wealth from the tangibles of gold, silver, and gems into the modern financial instruments of debt and credit, the weapons used by the Count to humiliate and destroy one of his enemies.

But the daydreams incited by stories like *The Count of Monte Cristo* played off the unforgiving, competitive realities of a world in which money and a market economy contaminated every aspect of social existence, including the most intimate spheres of family and personal life. A different category of nineteenth-century fiction, from Balzac to Trollope, Galdós, and James, continues to be relevant for its exposure of the chilling insinuation of money into human relationships. One reason these novels are revelatory is for how they observe the imposition of capitalist values at a time when vestiges of older, non-monetary codes and conduct still existed. By the mid-twentieth century, the full internalization of behaviors and needs shaped by capitalism often prevented its violence and toxicity from seeming noteworthy.

Flaubert's *Sentimental Education* (1869) has few equals for its pitiless account of how desires and hopes are warped in a society where money trumps everything. The aimless Frédéric Moreau opens a letter one morning: it's a legal notification that he is the sole heir of his uncle's sizable fortune. Instantly, he calculates the annual income from the estate and is transported envisioning the clothes, furnishings, gifts, and carriages that he can now afford. "The images flashed into his mind with such turbulence that he felt his head spinning." But his delirious anticipations are caused less by avarice and social ambition than for how this wealth will enable his infatuation with a married woman. Love and desire become contaminated with the efficacy of money. Among endless examples, we could also note Conrad's protagonist in *Almayer's Folly* (1895): an unsuccessful merchant in colonial Borneo whose love for his estranged daughter drives him to a futile quest for a lost gold mine in the forest, that would fund a triumphant return to Europe. The feverish pursuit of wealth becomes the imaginary remedy for his broken public and private life, motivated by an intermingling of love, greed, racism, and resentment.

Despite capitalism's penetration into so many layers of our lives, most of us know that it does not inevitably produce subjects who act solely out of self-interest and for private gain. However, in the absence of a society based on economic justice and responsibility for its members, the desire for wealth becomes the default pathway into which care and love for others is channeled. Beyond one's own wants and aspirations, empathy with the needs and deprivations of loved ones, whether children, partners, or friends, becomes tied to the impossible chance of an instant windfall with the lottery, online gambling, or other ventures. In Patti Smith's 1975 song, "Free Money," her narrator longs for the gratification that the winning ticket would bring: the ability to buy the things her lover needs or wants. Love's inescapable recourse to the illusions of money has been a core theme of popular culture for a century and a half.

Forms of magical thinking have always accompanied schemes for becoming wealthy, but, as some social theorists have shown, neoliberal globalization has spawned various "occult economies" almost everywhere.[33] The operations of finance capital pose the spectacle of wealth seemingly accumulated out of nothing, of value created without work or effort, prompting ordinary people to see "arcane forces" fueling the flows of money to the very rich. On every continent, there are hybrid prosperity religions, forms of divination, fortune telling, or ritual pyramid schemes in which mercenary hopes are invested. With its global availability, the internet complex has absorbed many of these occult economies and the emotions impelling them. Because everything that occurs on the limitless circuitry of the internet is quantified and therefore monetizable, many cling to a nebulous conviction that that online scalability holds the possibility of lottery-like riches for a commodified digital self. But the reality of the internet is its effectiveness in the channeling of the minuscule assets of the many into the portfolios of an elite few.

It is often said that billionaires are not the problem, that they are a secondary symptom of a market economy whose dynamics are not directly administered by anyone. However, even if this can be logically argued, the sociopathy of the global billionaire class (some soon to be trillionaires) produces a range of malignant consequences. A winner-take-all culture is not just incompatible with minimal norms of justice and democracy; it is synonymous with their disappearance. The unregulated, effectively lawless framework of global finance attracts and empowers a new category of criminals and psychopaths, especially now, with fewer or no constraints on the looting of social wealth and natural resources. As a result of the idolization of billionaires in mainstream media, those on the middle rungs of the class hierarchy must, in some way, adapt to this deranged social reality while those at the bottom of the global ladder are subjected to suffering, dispossession, and disposability.

We are a long way from the American "power elite" that C. Wright Mills observed in the 1950s. He described a loosely cohesive and self-replicating stratum within which disparities of wealth were compensated for by shared rituals of socialization and mobility within exclusionary institutional milieus. This class was also shaped by ideologies and political imperatives that inhibited the wholesale despoilment and sacking of their national economy and industries. Since then, globalization has enabled the emergence of a motley transnational billionaire coterie defined by net worth alone, freed up from most legal restraints and from responsibility to anything except what will expedite accumulation and enhance power. The institutional and spectacular forms through which billionaire culture is valorized and internalized constitute powerfully effective means of social control. An enormous gulf separates this lofty tier from the much larger meritocratic class of those who serve them, whether directly or otherwise. These are the zealous functionaries in banking, law, finance, media and entertainment conglomerates, design and fashion, research institutions and universities, technology companies of all kinds, and other sectors. Most of those in this demographic have no realistic expectation of becoming ultra-wealthy themselves, yet their allegiance to the super-rich is unshakable, stimulated by their intoxicating proximity to the spheres of exorbitant power and privilege. This superficially cosmopolitan class has a vassal-like relation to the uppermost elites, aware that subservient loyalty and contempt for sentiment or empathy will secure them a variety of benefits. The remaking of the world's major cities, in which the ostentatiousness of extreme wealth is woven into the physical fabric of urban space, serves to heighten one's imaginary relation to these rarified milieus and further strengthens obeisance. Yet, in spite of the urban incubation of this vassalage, these relationships play out in an extraterritoriality, divorced from any non-elite communities or larger social realities.

To reiterate, the wealth and power of the billionaire class are structurally interconnected with key elements of the internet complex. It's no coincidence that control of the dominant media and technology corporations are in the hands of this small elite. Most of the lucrative strategies of wealth production over the last two decades would have been inconceivable without the speeds and computational resources of advanced digital networks, the expansion of cryptocurrencies, of high-tech tax sheltering and money laundering schemes, and the permeability of profits from drugs, weapons, and human trafficking with more legitimate reservoirs of wealth. The massive relocation of social, economic, and personal life to online systems and platforms has propelled the ongoing upward transfer of wealth. With arrangements in which almost every gesture and glance can be monetized, it's inevitable that people are incited to be on screen 24/7. Thus, one of the ceaseless duties of the vassal class is to silence, exclude, or marginalize anyone questioning the social necessity and purported benefits of digital media products. They are the contemporary versions of the servile herd of writers and commentators, first noted by Karl Mannheim and Max Weber, whose primary function was, and remains today, the justification and consolidation of existing reality.

The facade of a "here to stay" system is defended ferociously against any refusals of corporate technological culture and the compulsory consumerism that supports it. Thanks to the watchdogs of the vassal class, the high-tech offerings of a handful of huge corporations are dissimulated as constituting an all-inclusive category of "technology," and even a partial shunning of them is twisted into opposition to any technology at all, or "wanting to return to nature." One of their priorities is to prevent exploration of how existing technical capabilities could be creatively redeployed by local and regional communities to meet human and environmental needs, rather than exclusively serving the requirements of capital and empire. The consistent portrayal of resistance to current technological arrangements as only a matter of a few isolated, disgruntled individuals reveals the actual fear shared by corporate plutocrats of large-scale, class-based refusals of the high-tech servitude imposed on labor. The straw man of a solitary technophobe is an anxious fiction to conceal the mass insurgent potential of millions of low-paid workers in Amazon warehouses, Walmarts, meat packing plants, call centers, and many other sites who are subjected to increasingly harsh regulation of their time and labor, and who also risk imminent replacement by robots. The unease of the elites is heightened by the many workplace struggles now erupting around the world, often targeting oppressive performance-related technologies.

During the last five years or so, as evidence of social disintegration has become impossible to ignore, there have been modifications in the oversight of mainstream commentary about digital technology and social media. It has become permissible, for example, to discuss particular negative consequences of various ways in which we use the internet and social media. However, anything deleterious must be presented as remediable within the continuing operation of global systems. Criticism can be framed in the reformist guise of the endless book titles or media content adhering to the same general formula of "How social media is a two-edged sword and how you can learn to use it to make your life and career more fulfilling and successful." "How Media Literacy Can Save Our Plugged-In World"; "Embrace the Good and Avoid the Bad in a Digital Age"; "How to Build a Healthy Relationship with Technology"; "Raising Kids to Thrive in a Connected World." On the other hand, any suggestion that a livable planet would necessitate a radical remaking of our lives, and a refusal of the products and services that drive the growth and wealth of mega-corporations, is unacceptable. It's important to recognize the more menacing implications of this recent spate of seemingly balanced formulations. Indirectly, they are a disavowal of the benign and egalitarian representations of the internet and a barely veiled warning that the internet complex, like every sphere of activity in late capitalism, is a competitive space occupied by a few winners and a great host of losers. The resources and benefits accessible online become defined by scarcity: that is, they are no longer immediately at hand, available to anyone. Now, as indebtedness, job insecurity, and unemployment intensify uncertainty and desperation, the revised message is that there are rewards obtainable on the internet, but they are on offer only to those who most fully conform to prescribed rules and market-based behaviors. Even for the diligent, of course, there is no guarantee of immunity from failure or disposability.

For the elites, the priority remains: keep people enclosed within the augmented unrealities of the internet complex, where experience is fragmented into a kaleidoscope of fleeting claims of importance, of never-ending admonitions on how to conduct our lives, manage our bodies, what to buy and who to admire or to fear. The separation and atomization of the internet is compounded by the humiliations and belittlements of billionaire culture. Unlike in earlier eras marked by extreme injustices and economic disparities, there is little ground for new solidarities to emerge around the realities and necessities of class conflict. In spite of ourselves, we capitulate to feelings of powerlessness or to illusory individual "solutions." Bloch's contention that the acquisitive drive appeared relatively recently at least holds the possibility that it could disappear again, or modulate into something else as social crises intensify. The sociologist Norbert Elias, however, provides a compelling supplement to the notion that drives and wishes have been continually changing throughout history. Writing on the estranging individualism endemic to Western modernity, he identified a human drive that was effectively trans-historical or innate. He insisted that the most basic human need "was for impulsive human warmth and spontaneity in relationships with other people . . . Whatever form it takes, the emotive need for human society, a giving and receiving in affective relationships to other people is one of the fundamental conditions of human existence."[34] The techno-modernists, no doubt, will tell us that human warmth is overrated, that to long for it is nostalgic and sentimental, and that there are all manner of apps and digital simulations to compensate us for its unavailability.

3

In our disintegrating society, the public sphere and the sphere
of intimacy atrophy at the same time.

Alexander Kluge

As the internet complex expands and aggregates, more facets of
our lives are funneled into the protocols of digital networks. The
disaster is the irredeemable incompatibility of online operations
with friendship, love, community, compassion, the free play of
desire, or the sharing of doubt and pain. Many of these disappear,
or they become recomposed into depleted simulations, drained
of their singularity and ineffability, permeated with absence and
shallowness. There is no joy or sorrow, no beauty or exuberance
on the internet. One can find poems, but no poetry. How can
we gauge the full consequences of so drastically confining the
richness and limitlessness of human potentiality within the
desolation and monotony of digital systems? The madness and
violence of this dissonance is evident everywhere, but at the same
time obscured by the delusional belief in the inevitability that
our lives must be lived online, where our hopes and creative
energies are inexorably dissipated.

In this sense, the internet complex is continuous with how capitalism has long demanded a channeling of human energies and emotions into patterns that are molded by economic and disciplinary requirements. Herbert Marcuse gave an influential account of this process: "Underlying the societal organization of human existence are basic libidinal wants and needs; highly plastic and pliable, they are shaped and coordinated with the interests of domination and thereby become a stabilizing force which binds the majority to the ruling minority."[1] Repression, he wrote, could become so effective that it took on the illusory form of freedom or independence, and one of his examples is the willing mass submission to the "entertainments" of the culture industry. Marcuse explained how the "performance principle" induced people to willingly perform pre-established kinds of labor or economically necessary functions instead of following their own desires or instincts. Central to his work was the contention that capitalism administers society through a fusion of technology and subjugation, of rationality and coercion. "Technology provides the great rationalization for the unfreedom of human beings and demonstrates the 'technical' impossibility of being autonomous, of determining one's own life."[2] At the same time, he argued that capitalism's exploitation of nature was damaging to human capacities for the sensuousness essential to the imagination and creation of non-oppressive social environments.

In the 1980s, postmodernists of various sorts dismissed Marcuse's work as old-fashioned: his understanding of power as repressive seemed heretical to all the newly minted Foucauldian academics. For others, he failed to recognize the "playful" and creative possibilities of technology. Then, after 1991, what did it all matter anyway, since capitalism was here to stay? Notwithstanding these critiques, Marcuse allows us to see some of the continuities of the internet complex with entrenched features of capitalism that have only intensified since the 1960s. More invasive forms of technical rationality have produced what Bernard Stiegler sees as an extreme phenomenon of proletarianization.[3] By this he means the ongoing colonization of consciousness, the homogenization of experience, and the anesthetization of the senses. Both worker and consumer are dispossessed—of knowledge, of communicative abilities, of desire.

In the mid-1930s, Edmund Husserl addressed the general outlines of the catastrophic predominance of technocratic values in modern European intellectual culture. In his unfinished text *The Crisis of European Sciences*, he put aside the rigorous formalism of his earlier work to examine what he saw as a tragic divide between modern science and the lifeworld. Then in his mid-seventies, writing after the enactment of the Nuremburg race laws, barred from teaching or publishing, Husserl's pessimism was compounded by his social isolation and deteriorating health. Nonetheless, *The Crisis* is only indirectly about the contemporary nightmare of Nazism. Rather, his concern is the "evil" and "barbarity" that result from one-sided rationalism, manifest in the mathematization of the world for objectives that betrayed a European dream of Reason guided by Spirit. For him, the crisis was the transformation of natural science into "mere technization." When mathematics "becomes a mere art of achieving results through a calculating technique according to technical rules, it no longer is grounded in the purposiveness of the life world."[4] Husserl provides numerous characterizations in ordinary language of what he means by *Lebenswelt*: it is "the world as the universal horizon common to all humans, of actually existing things . . . an openly endless horizon of human beings who are capable of meeting and then entering into actual contact with me and with one another." That is, the lifeworld is never private, it is the ongoing life and work of community, that occurs through what can be talked about with others. He insists that "in our continuously flowing world perceiving we are not isolated but rather have within it contact with other human beings . . . even what is straightforwardly perceptual is communalized."[5]

For Husserl, perception is a dynamic and constitutive element of common and shared experience. The lifeworld is ceaselessly recreated by the perceptual adjustments and attunements that ensue from the meeting of individuals in a communal milieu, a coming together marked by the rhythms of the day, of work and rest. Many others have also argued that the meeting, in Husserl's words "actual contact with others," is indispensable for the possibility of community and forms of democracy. Hannah Arendt championed the radicality of the workers' councils that first emerged during the French Revolution. These provisional expressions of self-government and egalitarian participation have appeared spontaneously during moments of crisis and upheaval, arising during the Paris Commune, in Europe between 1905 and 1919, in the 1956 Hungarian uprising, and in other moments. She also extolled the format of the New England town meeting, lamenting that this failed to take hold as America expanded westward.[6] The town meeting, quaint and outmoded as it may seem to some, is another manifestation of direct democracy, based on face-to-face decision-making, where people openly present who they are, in a non-hierarchical format. It was understandably feared and obstructed by James Madison and the early American elites. Together, the town meeting and councils pose a vision of small-scale community governance based on participation rather than passivity, where choices affecting the group are not left to representatives or experts.

Among economically disenfranchised peoples in southern Europe, Latin America, and other regions, informal neighborhood and workplace assemblies have emerged intermittently as forces for social and political change outside of established frameworks. A compelling example is the Zapatista movement in Mexico, which has grounded indigenous political struggles on traditional forms of direct democracy. Best known is their commitment to the *encuentro*, a community meeting, large or small, where debates of all kinds take place between equals. The format is privileged because it nurtures enduring forms of group interdependence and strengthens a sense of responsibility for collective decisions. This has not precluded the use of network technology for other kinds of communication, but these have been secondary to the shared exchanges of the *encuentro*.

Readers of Guy Debord's *Society of the Spectacle* often pass over his admiration for workers' councils and his advocacy of the council form as a vital element of revolutionary struggles. In the concluding paragraph, he writes that the power of the councils was "the realization of that active, direct communication which marks the end of all specialization, all hierarchy and all separation." Debord was one of many for whom the encounter *(rencontre)* was essential for resisting the spectacle's suspension of a common lifeworld. The spectacle, he wrote, produces "a systematic organization of a breakdown in the faculty of encounter and the replacement of that faculty by a social hallucination, an illusion of encounter." It's not difficult to see the internet complex as continuous with developments that were well underway in the 1960s, but today's social media perform an even more sweeping eradication of community.

While forms of mediated communication have existed for millennia, it's only recently that tele-phonic and tele-visual apparatuses have become fully integrated extensions of the ways we communicate. Most of these developed in response to the needs of a growing global economy and a modernizing military, but, until the mid-twentieth century, they remained supplemental to long-standing patterns of direct meetings and encounters between human beings. As Debord and others noted, spontaneous or unprogrammed forms of being together became irreconcilable with the rationalization of consumer society. This led to the suppression of uncontrolled political or popular assemblies and to the commodification of the urban spaces and temporalities of everyday life in which ordinary forms of personal interaction occurred. The techno-modernists have long disparaged any attachment to in-person interaction, insisting on its irrelevance amid all the new tools for "communicating." But the unspoken truth is that face-to-face encounters entail too much wasted time to be compatible with the speeds and financial efficiencies of online exchange and no data can be extracted from them and instantly put to use.

The value of a face-to-face encounter has nothing to do with some misplaced sense of its authenticity compared to telematics or other kinds of remote contact, which have their own authentic features. Rather, the direct encounter between human beings is something other than and incomparable with the exchange or transmission of words, images, or information. It is always suffused with non-linguistic and non-visual elements. Even when unexceptional or unmindful, the face-to-face meeting is an irreducible basis of the lifeworld and its commonality; it is charged with the possible emergence of something unforeseen that has nothing to do with normative communication. An encounter does not occur in empty space, nor is it bounded by the frame of a screen. It is an immersion, an inhabiting of an atmospherics, affecting every sense, whether consciously or not. This kind of meeting, this proximity, is literally a con-spiracy, a breathing together.

Yet the stifling of our propensity for encounters and their responsibilities unfolds on many levels. One of the forces exacerbating this debilitation is the pervasive use of biometric procedures and related techniques to reconfigure human behavior and responses into quantifiable information. There is little in the body and brain that is not now subjected to extraordinary forms of monitoring and analysis, and an important goal of this data acquisition is to maximize and habitualize our use of network technology. During the last decade, biometrics have been debated and critiqued extensively but mostly around questions of surveillance, consumer profiling, and digital policing. My concern in this chapter, however, is the fate of what makes possible and sustains an intersubjective lifeworld: the voice, the face, and the gaze. Capitalism requires their appropriation and utilization as part of the weakening of an individual's capacity for caring, empathy, or community. Biometrics furthers the comprehensive habituation of human beings to interfacing with machine systems. The reductiveness of its operations, especially when these target vision and speech, leads to a splintering of the interhuman basis of a shared social reality.

Biometrics grew out of the need for information about ill-defined urban populations, especially in relation to the organization of labor and new forms of policing and control. Social modernization required that individuals be knowable, visible, and identifiable. The laboratory-based research known as "psycho-physics" was based on the principle that any relevant information about a human subject was obtainable through external quantitative methods. Everything once associated with psychological interiority, such as mind or consciousness, was taken to have a measurable physiological basis. This was part of the origin of what historian Andreas Bernard calls "the quantified self."[7]

By the 1880s, one area of research was the functioning of attentiveness. It became important to determine its capabilities and limits, to learn how many things someone could pay attention to simultaneously, and what enhanced concentration or led to distraction. Initially these studies examined the attentiveness of workers in assembly-line production and, by the early twentieth century, the effectiveness of advertising, teaching methods, or any labor that depended on alertness or vigilance.[8] This furthered the growth of enterprises that would develop into the eye tracking industries of the present. Cumbersome machines began to be used in the 1930s, but now miniaturization has allowed eye tracking software to be embedded in almost any device or location. Because so much economic activity depends on the constant use of digital interfaces (in schools, the workplace, the military, entertainment and gaming), it's obvious why the eye is now a major site of data gathering. High-tech corporations model their ambitions around an "attention economy" in which financial success requires soliciting the greatest number of "eyeballs." Just as time-motion studies and scientific management techniques sought to make efficient the motions and work of the body during a key phase of industrial capitalism, now scrutiny of the eye serves the goal of managing an observer's vision and training the eye to be an accessory of information processing.

Not until the late nineteenth century did eye movement become an object of sustained study. The French researcher Émile Javal is credited with the first account, in the 1880s, of what he famously termed the "saccadic" movements of the human eye. The connotations of this French word suggest a jerky, halting,

fits-and-starts movement, and it's in the context of industrial
modernity that such a characterization became possible. For
thousands of years, close observers of other people were aware
of the vital motility of the eye. Yet in the rich and diverse accounts
of the eye and vision by Aristotle, Alhazen, Roger Bacon,
Al-Kindi, Leonardo, Kepler, and many others, the movement
identified by Javal is of little or no interest. Even in the geometrical modeling of sight by Dürer and Brunelleschi, there was
never any incompatibility between the tremulousness of the eye
and quantifiable conceptions of visual perception. But with the
advent of environments saturated with many forms of repetitive
and unfaltering machine motion, the natural activity of the eye,
like other behaviors of the body, came to seem erratic or hap-
hazard in comparison, and in need of correction.

However, it is through the restless, rapid movement of our
eyes (ten to twenty times per second) that we continually create
our visual world. Because only a small central area of the retina
registers with acute clarity, most of what our eye sees is indistinct
and vague. By constantly shifting that delimited zone of clarity,
we synthesize an illusory but coherent picture of an external
reality that appears as present to us. Eye movement is the temporal encounter of a body with a world in a state of continual
emergence, an encounter in which memory, perception, and other
senses seamlessly cooperate. Our eyes skim the surfaces of the
world around us, motivated by a welter of interests, expectations,
anxieties, and desires. For the philosopher Henri Bergson, an
observer could never be understood as "a mathematical point in
space." A human being, he insisted, was a living "center of inde-
termination," a position from which the world was perpetually
changing, open to action, choice, and the possibility of freedom.
Whatever minimized this indeterminacy or rendered perception

habitual was an inhibition of life. Bergson was followed by many others over the next century, who sought to resist the standardization of perception and the regulation of attention required by the industrialization of labor and new visual technologies. Eye tracking is currently one part of this larger and ongoing project of colonization.

Many assume that eye tracking is an intrusive form of biometric surveillance that identifies and archives the details of what we look at. But spying on individuals and their personal proclivities is not one of its main objectives. A more important goal is the discovery of large-scale regularities among targeted demographics, with the aim of financializing the harvested information. Eye tracking data is used to curtail some of the intrinsic incompatibilities between human vision and the visual milieus we now inhabit, and it provides analytics needed by designers for steering sight into appropriately attentive behaviors. The accumulated knowledge about the motor activity of the eye (literally, the rotation of the eyeballs), is processed and deployed to maximize the likelihood of a user "attending" to pre-designed points or sequences of visual attraction. Put another way: the more that is known about the typical patterns of eye movements, what a gaze is drawn to and what it avoids, the easier it is to contrive visual attractions that will successfully solicit or engage visual attention. Thus, the actual use of eye tracking devices is merely the means by which data is acquired, and whether any individual user has ever been "tracked" is irrelevant. Our concern should be that we are all increasingly inhabiting and interacting with online worlds fabricated to effect predetermined, routinized visual responses.

According to one of the leading global firms, eye tracking provides "compelling objective data that reveals the human behavior behind the interaction with interfaces or products *and uncovers optimization potential*."[9] In one sense, it resembles older projects of persuasion—inducing us to look at or purchase something while maintaining the illusion that we are choosing and acting autonomously. Eye tracking records many phenomena, but one of the most important is the pattern established between the movements of the eyeball and the intervals of relative immobility, which are called fixations. The erroneous assumption among designers of eye tracking software is that if the eye is directed at a particular location, even for a very short time, then this constitutes attention. A parallel and equally flawed assumption is that there is a correlation between what one is looking at and what one is thinking. Thus, for the needs of digital marketing and other business sectors, the complexities of attentiveness are reduced to a physiological model of brief and disconnected intervals of motor fixation of the eyeball.

Eye tracking analytics are especially important in the expansive industry of user experience design, known as UXD. This rapidly expanding business sector is responsible for much of what we see online and for the narrow models of attention that are the basis for their design work. One company tells potential clients, "We're looking to create emotional connections in our design of tax preparation and personal finance websites. If you create an experience that connects with a user on an emotional level, you've succeeded." IBM, like most big corporations, does all their UXD in-house. In their "cognitive e-commerce" division, the stated goal is to build "deeper human engagement . . . By knowing what our customers want before they do, by understanding nuances of tone, sentiment and environmental conditions, we can engage customers on a human level and deliver the right experience at the perfect moment to inspire lifelong advocacy."

One UXD firm announces that they have fashioned "magical and meaningful payment experiences" for shopping websites. Most often the goal of UXD is to craft interfaces that are "frictionless, effortless, smooth," but which produce dutiful and pliant consumers. Here, "frictionless" is a synonym for the absence of reflection, thought, or doubt.

William James, in his *Principles of Psychology*, made a concise and provisional definition: "experience is what I agree to attend to," while UXD is the perversion of this maxim into "experience is what we tell you to attend to." James deplored the reduction of attention to a mechanism divested of intentionality and insisted that it could and should have an ethical dimension, established by the choices and self-aware priorities of the individual. For him, a common field of experience took shape through the willed attentiveness of a historically evolving community of individuals. John Dewey went further in his extended accounts of the importance of experience as heightened vitality, as "a complete interpenetration of self and the world." Experience, he said, happens not merely in an environment, but because of it, through interaction with it. It was like breathing, "a rhythm of intakings and outgivings." For Dewey, experience was fundamentally transactional; he rejected the notion that it was the subjective product of private consciousness. Rather, the ebb and flow of life occurred in social milieus where "experience is the greatest of human goods . . . a sharing whereby meanings are enhanced, deepened and solidified in the sense of communion."[10]

Dewey's failure here was his inability to see the incompatibility between his vivid evocation of the creative potential of social experience, and the tedious functionalism of the institutions he believed indispensable to economic and scientific progress. Now, however, the possibility of a common life of direct experience has been replaced by a passive receptivity to streams of stimuli that are imposed on us non-consensually. Again, the result is not so much new forms of control, which are rarely as effective as purported, but the impairing of our ability or even desire to make perceptual discriminations in real living environments. Long disparaged by academic philosophers, experience is the most accessible frame for ordinary people to articulate how the current order inflicts unhappiness on them, anxiety, indebtedness, ill health, loneliness, addiction, and worse. As William Blake understood, it is when experience becomes a hell that one recognizes the necessity of radically transforming the conditions of work, life, and imagination.[11]

Eye tracking is an essential tool for UXD designers because it indicates what features in a display or controlled environment are most "eye-catching." Usually this correlates to what is recorded as a user's "first fixation." This is simultaneously cross-referenced with "gaze time," blinks, scrolling and clicking patterns, and other layers of information. The priority is not just to direct a viewer to a particular visual object but also to channel our visual engagement from one fixation to another. It's important that nothing be looked at for very long, which is why there is a sequencing of attractions that briefly hold the "gaze point" but then lead elsewhere. Paradoxically, an "eye-catching" visual object is also one that is shallow and without complexity. It must have some features that are perceptually compelling but quickly drained of interest. Equally important is how eye tracking identifies and helps in the elimination of anything deemed confusing. These would be design elements endowed with some degree of ambiguity, indistinctness, unintelligibility, or other quality that would frustrate an immediate or effortless perceptual grasp. Eye tracking would detect a hesitancy, a kind of "stammering" of eye movement that, even relatively briefly, is unable to settle into a secure fixation. But such minor sources of visual uncertainty and vagueness are corrected or removed in order to optimize "usability."

However, ambiguity and indistinctness are fundamental for our ability to make visual discriminations of many kinds. It would take too long to name all the artists, poets, and thinkers on the subject of sight in the last 500 years, from Leonardo, Rembrandt, and Goethe through Ruskin, Emerson, William James, and Mallarmé, for whom indistinctness and obscurity are fundamental elements of visual experience as they straddle the boundaries between vision, the flux of memory, and the creativity of reverie. Today, however, engaging imaginatively with perplexing visual information is incompatible with the efficient integration of the viewer into the duties and temporalities set by neoliberal institutions. Thus, the most disturbing consequences of eye tracking have less to do with surveillance and privacy than with the devaluation and routinization of vision.

One of the broader goals of eye tracking is the training of an observer-user into probable patterns of performativity. Anything that encourages prolonged attention or even partially contemplative states is unacceptable because of the indefinitely longer amount of time such a response might take up. At the same time, eye movement that is vacillating or "aimless" is behavior to be deterred or redirected. We often assume that internet "surfing" means the possibility of following random, uncharted visual itineraries but, in most instances, this is only a pseudo-wandering that is, in fact, tracing a predictable sequence of fixation points interspersed with habitual patterns of scrolling and clicking. Like the phrase "to navigate a website," surfing connotes an open, aqueous milieu, but the reality is repetitive itineraries devoid of actual drift or waywardness. From the standpoint of the bored individual, hours spent in this way may seem to be a desultory waste of time, but it is time occupied in a contemporary mode of informal work that produces value as marketable information for corporate and institutional interests. The eye (and mind) is discouraged from being errant and the observer is prevented from getting lost, or from evading requisite visual tasks.

In one sense, eye tracking is part of the persistence of what William Blake called "single vision," which he linked to the narrowness of a Newtonian understanding of physical reality and a Lockean model of sensation. One of his best-known images depicts Newton using the two-pointed arms of a compass to trace a geometrical diagram. Staring fixedly at the confined space of what is "encompassed" by the instrument he holds, Newton sits blinkered from the overwhelming sensory plurality of the world, tragically cut off from the visionary powers inherent in all human beings. For Blake, single vision was the merely mechanical activity of the eye, isolated from interplay with the other senses and the imagination. The separation of the senses, which Marx was also to describe, became an integral part of the industrialization of perception that took off in the later nineteenth century. The filmmaker Stan Brakhage, who was influenced by Blake's mythopoetic framework, saw a related constriction of the senses in contemporary techniques for the management of vision, well before the internet: "Most people's eyes are caught in tricks imposed by some very greedy people, so they move along certain channels of *prescribed* light. And the way they get tricked is that they don't look at the qualities and varieties of light. They're only trained to use it as something bouncing off objects, or papers, or signs; finally, even the objects cease to exist."[12]

Eye tracking, in its actual workings as much as in its name, parallels the relation between hunter and hunted. It's a technology of pursuit with the goal of capture, as the phrase "eye-catching" confirms. With each new generation of digital displays, there are fewer possibilities of the eye remaining fugitive or autonomous. Specific features reinforce the affinity of eye tracking with hunting as well. The beam of light projected by an LED onto the pupil and iris is a targeting of the eye's radial structure, a literal target composed of concentric circles. Along with many new firearms and other weapons, eye tracking targets the observer with infrared light (IR). The human eye cannot see infrared wavelengths and therefore the body does not respond protectively by shutting the eyelid or turning the head away as one would in reaction to intense white light or sunlight. It produces no "aversion" response and it does not cause the pupil to contract, which also facilitates the gathering of data. Not only is it light that is not seen but it produces heat that is not felt. Infrared light raises the internal temperature of the eye, actually "baking" it and injuring the tissue. Medical studies indicate that IR exposure can lead to cataracts, corneal ulcers and retinal burns. Not coincidentally, this aspect of eye tracking corresponds to features of so-called directed-energy weapons, which deploy selected wavelengths of the spectrum to harm or destroy.

Evolution over tens of thousands of centuries has shaped the eye's sensitivity to the energy of natural light; the anatomy of the eye was formed to collect and focus light of certain wavelengths on the retina. For most of human history visible light, in all its various conceptualizations, was the only known part of the spectrum. Premodern cultures, with few exceptions, were shaped by a primal awareness of light as a form of energy that interacts powerfully with matter, most evident in the dependency of plant life on the sun. Its apparent immateriality yet luminous sensual immediacy allowed it to play a decisive role in the cosmologies of almost every society. Light was understood to possess transformative powers that were consistently spiritual or regenerative. But, in the West, during the nineteenth century, visible light loses its ontological privilege and from a scientific standpoint ceases to have an independent identity, as it becomes conceptualized and manipulated as an electromagnetic phenomenon.

Many overlook the fateful consequences of the rapid discovery of what is generally accepted today as the electromagnetic spectrum. From 1886 to 1914, there was a quickening accumulation of research developments that led to some of the foundations of the techno-political-social world we inhabit more than a century later. A cursory outline of those years would include the work of Hertz (radio waves), Roentgen (X-rays), Becquerel and the Curies (radioactivity), Villard and then Rutherford and Bohr (gamma rays). However, these discoveries and their irrevocable remaking of visibility did not occur fortuitously or as part of some disinterested quest for greater scientific knowledge. This familiar constellation of names sustains the popular narrative of theoretical and practical breakthroughs made by individual geniuses. But the reality is of gifted individuals working within what Max Weber identified as "state-capitalist enterprises," that is, within the new institutional complexes specific to the nation states then competing for territorial and economic domination on a global scale.[13] The annexation of the electromagnetic spectrum coincided with the professionalization and specialization of science and with the demands of militarism, economic growth, and imperial expansion for new forms of energy, communication, and destruction. Of course, one of the most important developments of that 1886–1914 period was the research on the radioactive properties of uranium. Through multiple pathways, these discoveries would culminate over two decades later with the discovery of nuclear fission and the making of an atomic bomb. Now, in the twenty-first century, most of life takes place in a saturated field of non-visible radiant energy, including the wireless networks whose radio waves reshape more and more facets of personal and institutional life. Most importantly, these developments have led to the industries of social control and mass lethal violence based on the vulnerability of the body and its defenselessness against scanning, monitoring, targeting, and irradiation. This condition of exposedness robs human perception of the possibility of being an opening and a facing onto the world, and instead amplifies the status of the eye as a site of external intervention.

Iris scanning is another technology often aligned in the same devices with eye tracking. It, too, uses invisible infrared light to produce a digital image of superior precision to images made with visible light. It is one of the many forms of biometric identification being marketed and deployed internationally. The human iris fulfills the standard requirements for a biometric marker: universality (everyone has one), permanence (it doesn't change over a lifetime), uniqueness (every iris is different), and accessibility (to being recorded). This use of the iris was actually first proposed by one of the originators of biometric procedures, the Parisian police official Alphonse Bertillon. In an 1892 research paper, he noted the potential usefulness of the iris as a biomarker, even though he knew that contemporary image-making techniques were inadequate for its implementation.[14] It wasn't until the 1990s that iris scanning products became widely available and, as of 2016, more than a billion images have been made.

Until the very recent past, the exterior of the eye, with the
iris its most vivid feature, had cultural meaning as a defining
element of human face-to-face encounters. For thousands of
years, in many different cultures, the iris was the presence in
the body of a flickering chromatic vivacity, akin to natural
phenomena such as rainbows or flowers. However, unlike the
fleeting occurence of a rainbow or the transience of flowers, the
iris persists in the body for a lifetime. A shared gaze always holds
the promise of a glimpse of iridescence, whether between friends,
lovers, or strangers. Neither opaque nor transparent, the iris and
its elusive colors shimmer and in their gentle dazzlement some
mystery at the heart of the other is withheld. It is moreover the
iris, with its contractile muscles, that constantly adjusts the size
of the pupil to control the amount of light entering the eye. It
has a rhythmic response to the illumination or darkening of the
world. Amid the fluctuations of light, the appearance of the iris,
its aqueous translucence, modulates and resists chromatic stabi-
lization. How often have we noticed of someone we know well
that the color of their eye shifts in different light? A wonder of
the iris is that, for an observer, it is never identical to itself: its
colors are not static and thus unpossessable. Hegel, in his *Lectures
on Art*, remarked on the singular brilliance of the iris and declared
that it could never be authentically depicted in art.

However, some artists were not deterred from attempting to
approximate the beauty of the iris. Art historian Hanneke
Grootenboer has examined a short-lived trend in the late eight-
eenth and early nineteenth centuries of miniature paintings of
a single eye.[15] These framed, often bejeweled, watercolors on
ivory were exchanged between lovers and family members as
private, sentimental portraits, worn as pendants or brooches.
They depict the full eye and eyebrow, but the chromatic rendering

of the iris is key to their effectiveness. Grootenboer sees these artifacts as evidence of an alternate model of visuality in which the reciprocity of gazes is experienced with extraordinary closeness. It is what she calls "an intimate vision" in which contemplation of the other's eye opens onto both its cherished familiarity and its enigmatic beauty. The ecologist Paul Shepard noted the evolutionary importance of the human eye with its iris as an organ of communication, in addition to its receptive functions. "The colored iris set in a white background is one of the most compelling features of human physiognomy."[16] Between people in the act of self-presentation, eyes give and receive information; he further observes that apes, dogs, and even some birds are attracted to the human eye and iris. "More than any other single factor, eye communication transcends the profound barriers of communication between species."

The Swiss zoologist Adolf Portmann offered a broader framework in which to consider the color of the iris. Rejecting functionalist explanations based on natural selection, Portmann proposed that "the appearance of every living organism serves a fundamental purpose: self-expression or self-projection."[17] Years of research led him to the stunning hypothesis that the living world, in its infinite richness of color and form, "is designed to be seen." Writing in the 1950s, when positivist assumptions about the study of nature went mostly unquestioned, Portmann sought a holistic understanding of the sensory interconnectedness of an animate earth. At the same time, he was one of a few deploring the spread of a visual illiteracy brought on by reproductive media (such as *National Geographic* and TV wildlife shows) and exclusively urban lifestyles, resulting in remoteness from a non-human lifeworld. Since then, the estrangement of our senses from the world has been immeasurably heightened by the pervasiveness of computer-generated images of all kinds. Now, for example, we can easily access magnified, ultra-high-resolution images of irises which reveal countless details unseen in a direct meeting— yet for most viewers these become unremarkable curiosities, drained of anything experienced in lived, interpersonal proximity.

One particular capability of eye tracking is the collection of data on what colors and combinations of colors and graphics are most or least eye-catching, information that is then deployed in the management of perception and response. Research on color and behavior, especially in relation to advertising, is hardly new, but what has changed is our 24/7 engagement with the chromatic environment of screens and displays. The ubiquity of electro-luminescence has crippled our ability or even motivation to see, in any close or sustained way, the colors of physical reality. Habituation to the glare of digital displays has made our perception of color indifferent and insensitive to the delicate evanescence of living environments. For tens of thousands of years, human life was lived around the ceaseless rhythm of day turning into night into day. Every morning was a flowering and recoloring of the world after an interval of sometimes moonlit or starlit darkness. However, the nocturnal suspension of color is not an objective reality. The photoreceptors in our eyes that enable us to see color cannot function in low light, and the rods that enable us to see in near darkness are insensitive to colors. Thus, the pulse of this endless coloring and darkening is an experience specific to our body's response to the daily rotation of the earth. This is why twilight has always been a unique part of those passages from day to night. Dusk is an interval that heightens our sensitivity to the transition from direct solar radiance to the indirect and slowly dwindling illumination of the sky. It's a time when the deepening of colors can be felt with all our senses.

Color is continuous with our tactile sensitivity to inflections in the air, to sounds, odors, and to a bodily awareness that birds, animals, and vegetation are likewise attuned to this daily event. During all the thousands of years of premodernity and prehistory, what we think of as color would never have been separable from this interplay of the senses and from the vital presence of other coexisting forms of life. [18] Only in the last several centuries, beginning in the West, has the reduction of color to exclusively optical properties taken place, and the fragmentary notion of a sunset or landscape become possible as a detached visual spectacle for a distanced observer.

The invention of artificial colors in the mid-nineteenth century had far-reaching consequences. It's no coincidence that the large-scale manufacture of highly profitable synthetic dyes, in the 1860s, brought into being the chemical conglomerates, from IG Farben and BASF to Dow, Dupont, and Sinopec, that have been damaging and obliterating life on the planet for the last hundred years. The industrialization of color is historically inter-twined with the making of plastics, herbicides, pesticides, PCBs, polyvinyl chloride, and innumerable other compounds that have poisoned our water, air, soils, and oceans. Driven by the expansion of commodity production and the rise of mass consumption, the proliferation of manufactured color is part of a larger relocation of sensory experience into the needs and values of a capitalist economy. Synthetic color becomes allied with techniques of attraction, solicitation, and persuasion. Writing around 1900, the sociologist Georg Simmel observed that when nothing is exempt from becoming monetized or exchangeable we are condemned to a world drained of color, stripped of the fabric woven from all the moments of heightened life and quiet elation that are born most often in mutuality and intimacy. "To the extent that money, with its colorlessness (*Farbenloskeit*) and indifferent quality, can become a common denominator of all values, it becomes the frightful leveler—it hollows out the core of things, their peculiarities, their specific values and their uniqueness and incomparability in a way that is beyond repair."[19]

Simmel's piercing characterization remains fitting for our own present where we are enveloped in the algorithmic nullity of electroluminescence. We are rendered incapable of directly apprehending the fragile interconnectedness of all living things. 24/7 engagement with screens has so thoroughly anesthetized us that we've lost the sensory capacity to experience ourselves as part of the animate matrix of earthly life.[20] As David Abram and others have warned, we've lost our bodily understanding of the world and its rhythms and no longer have a kinesthetic immersion in living environments.[21] We may abstractly deplore the millions of lives and species rendered disposable by capitalism or the devastation of ecosystems on which we depend, but we cling to our disembodied online routines and to the illusion that the internet complex is somehow not a primary agent of the catastrophe.

Many believe that our main concern should be with the intrusive, privacy-violating objectives of biometrics. However, the current clamor over "surveillance capitalism" needs to be made transparent: its target is not capitalism, but the supposed excesses and violations that have been imposed on a fundamentally reformable but indispensable system. It is a deflection of critique that affirms the permanence and necessity of the existing underlying arrangements. The intensifying of our anxiety about online privacy, corporate data mining, and threats like malware and DoS attacks, only deepens our investment in the logic of social separation and in the paranoid premises of cyber security. By design, there never will be network privacy for individuals; but we are nonetheless asked to believe that legislation to guarantee privacy may someday happen, that current abuses can be curbed, and that we can reclaim the reassuring fiction of "our" internet that in fact never existed. We are pushed further into identifying ourselves with our data, our search history, our passwords. The demands of secrecy, anonymization, encryption, and firewalls warp every aspect of our online lives and undermine the sustaining of democratic or communitarian values. Cyber security and the weariness of endless upgrades become a normalized part of daily life. One IT security firm promotes its products as follows: "The new threatscape we all inhabit requires zero trust. Zero trust security assumes that bad actors already exist both inside and outside the network. Trust must therefore be entirely removed from the equation."

Facial recognition is one of the core technologies of the global biometrics industry and much of the critical debate around it has concerned privacy, inaccurate identifications, racialized bias, and its use in "social credit" ratings. However, in addition to the identification of a specific individual through matching with an archived "faceprint," there are other significant uses of these resources, especially in emotion recognition technology or what is called "affective computing." One major company offers software for "seamless data collection, synchronization, visualization and analysis in combination with other sensors and technologies such as eye tracking, galvanic skin response, EEG, facial expression analysis, and much more in one single computer system." One of the aims is to determine the emotional state of someone under observation, often through the categories of happiness, sadness, surprise, anger, fear, disgust, and contempt, and dozens of secondary expressions. Corporations, with names like

Affectiva, Emotient, and *Beyond Verbal,* are developing forms of
"facial coding" or "Emotion AI" to analyze facial expressions in
real time. In the words of one company's promotions, "we now
have a powerful way to understand consumers' unfiltered
responses," by measuring moment-by-moment reactions to digital
video and ads. For example, it can identify the ads that generate
the best emotional response on repeat viewings, or the on-screen
behaviors of media personalities that draw viewers back. Equally
important is the use of these applications in gaming design in
order to maximize addictiveness. Again, as I insisted in my
discussion of eye tracking, the consequences of affective computing have begun to diminish all of our lives, regardless of whether
we have ever been individually subjected to these techniques.
They are one aspect of the reductive homogenization and mech-
anization of emotion which neoliberal capitalism requires.

Analysis of the smile is particularly important for the design
of products or content that aims to provoke a pleasurable
response. There is software capable of detecting all kinds of
smiles, especially to indicate when a minimum "smile threshold"
is triggered by stimuli of various kinds. This computational
scrutiny of the face can also interpret micro-expressions, such as
the flickers of involuntary motor activity that, for example, might
conceal the expression of an emotion or simulate an emotion we
do not feel. There are scanners for detecting asymmetric facial
expressions such as slight traces of smirks or grimaces. Unlike
symmetric smiles which are deemed to indicate happiness and
enjoyment, asymmetric smiles (with lips higher on one side of
the face) supposedly disclose a "negative valence" which might
include emotions such as consternation, defiance, or skepticism.
At the same time, computer analysis of the smile is an important
tool for the design of robots or digital avatars in order to endow

them with credible and seemingly genuine expressions. In the words of one robotics company, the goal is "to infuse them with emotional intelligence and make them truly social." What was once part of the vital background fabric of everyday life, that is, the ways we present ourselves to others, is relocated into numbing and debasing functions. As we expand our interactions with machines as a face, a voice or both, vacuous models of emotion and expression begin to pervade an immense number of situations. The point is not that we are becoming like machines or behaving inauthentically. Rather, we're on the verge of losing the ability or even the interest in engaging the gaze or voice of another as an object of care or intimate reflection.

Historians Jean-Jacques Courtine and Claudine Haroche have shown how the face, in the West, has been a contested site around which different practices of self-presentation have developed.[22] As modern notions of individuality emerged, especially in the seventeenth century, the face, with all its expressive possibilities, required self-mastery and control. Because the face could potentially reveal and expose one, it was important to learn ways of rendering it opaque or inscrutable. New social environments demanded the ability to modulate one's expression to conceal real feelings or to simulate false ones. Beginning in court society, individuals learned what facial expressions were appropriate to specific social situations and what was permissible in private, more intimate settings. During this same period, knowledge was produced that offered ways of understanding and deciphering expression. However, for Courtine and Haroche, the availability of photography and the advent of mass society in the later nineteenth century changed everything. The ubiquity of photographic images, in media of all kinds, the emergence of new regularities and typologies, and the anonymity and atomization of modern urban life diminished the relevance of what was derivable from direct encounters.

Over a century later, with the ascendance of the neurosciences, social media, and the AI capabilities just surveyed, there has been a foreclosure of individual attentiveness to what social theorist Avery Gordon describes as "complex personhood."[23] The billions of images of faces in online advertising and on social media, most of them smiling, make up a limitless, disheartening surface defined by a narrow yet vague attribute of "likeability." Of course, this is reciprocally related to the vast enterprise of corporate face and voice recognition: a scrutiny primarily undertaken to determine and enhance the attractiveness of services and products. What is most disturbing is not the commodification of sentiment or the ominous scenario of behavior control. Rather, it is the wreckage of social formations in which understanding and experience of others, of the uniqueness and indeterminacies of faces and voices, were once valued. We are losing the ability to see a face or hear a voice in its temporal depth, to apprehend the signs and sounds of experiences gathered over a lifetime. The critic Sigrid Weigel has written about how the deep traces of loss, sorrow, love, perseverance, or resignation in a human face are superfluous, hence illegible, to machine emotion analysis.[24] More importantly, these imprints of a life with which we all are marked are becoming increasingly imperceptible for anyone habituated to amnesiac and quasi-automated online exchanges.

Ever since the early twentieth century, the face has been a theme of critical and ethical significance. In the context of both the increasing fragmentation of urban life and of World War I with its millions of slaughtered and maimed, the face invited a new valuation and even sanctification, evident in various ways in the writings of Georg Simmel, Rainer Maria Rilke, Max Picard, Martin Buber, Franz Rosenzweig, and later, after World War II, in the work of Emmanuel Levinas. But, within the contested ideological field of the first decades of the twentieth century, any defense of the uniqueness of the individual within mass society or reflection on the notion of personhood were often dismissed as bourgeois humanism or anti-modern disillusionment. However, amid the ongoing incorporations of the face into the functioning of digital surveillance, marketing, and vacuous social media, some of those earlier meditations resonate with continued relevance. There is a long history of the face-as-image, whether of Christ, of whiteness, of the monarch or tyrant. By the early twentieth century the despotism of the face had been assimilated into dominant forms of spectacle and celebrity culture, but within this oppressive continuum of face-as-image, the living face of the suffering, the destitute, or the non-white is consistently erased.

For Martin Buber, the face was important as a defining element of a human encounter in which speech (or the withholding of speech) was made possible. At the heart of life, for Buber, was the actuality of a meeting that occasioned dialogue or held forth its possibility. Dialogue was crucial to the building or sustaining of living together as a community. His evolving advocacy of a communitarian socialism came out of his sustained engagement with the work of Proudhon, Marx, Kropotkin, Landauer, and Lenin, as well as with the experiences of the Paris Commune, workers' cooperatives, and the early kibbutzim. Working and being together required from everyone a level of shared responsibility, but this could only occur meaningfully as a response to what *faces* one in a living situation. Thus, one was obliged to resist engaging with the face as image or listening to speech out of habit. The glance, Buber says, "lives in the space of events." Every living situation has a new face that has never been and will never come again.

Contrary to some mischaracterizations of Buber's work, there is nothing mystical or blandly warm-hearted about his notion of the meeting. Meetings can occur between strangers or enemies as much as between neighbors, co-workers, or lovers, between two people or within a group; the meeting is simply an inescapable precondition for the sustaining of human connectedness: "even violence against a being one truly encounters is better than ghostly solicitude for faceless digits."[25] Dialogue opens up, not to some Rousseauian meeting of souls, but to the contingent possibility of "living, reciprocal relationships" in a shattered world. As Buber was to insist, mutuality would always be incomplete, never fully achieved, just as the community of which it was the foundation was always an unfinished and ongoing project. Buber readily acknowledged that we spend most of our lives in the "It-world" of institutions and markets where the desire for gain and the will to power are natural and inevitable forces. But, throughout history, the depersonalized "It-world" had been mitigated by communal forms of life in which caring, mutual support, and festivity were valued and sustained. Yet technological modernity, he feared, was so encroaching on those spheres that "the interhuman is threatened in its very existence."[26]

The value of Buber's work lies not in the degree of its originality but in the clarity with which it articulates what is intuitively known or apprehended by many; it has the familiarity and epiphanic force of the commonplace. This is also why Buber continues to be patronized or dismissed by many academic philosophers for whom his accessibility is a disqualification. They

compare him unfavorably with Emmanuel Levinas, whose ethical theory is extolled, in part, for its "challenging" abstruseness.
Enlightening for Buber, as it has been for other thinkers, was
the Heraclitus fragment, "The waking have one world in
common." Now, with the dispossession and instrumentalization
of the face, voice, and gaze there is a further disabling of the
most basic capablities through which the common can be
invoked.

Giorgio Agamben, writing in the early 1990s, anticipated this
sweeping dispossession as the closing down of the very possibility
of dialogic speech, as violence to "the linguistic being of humans."
He, too, cites Heraclitus's "one world in common" to preface his
account of the effects of global media and information networks:
"What is being appropriated is the possibility itself of a common
good."[27] Writing before the widespread diffusion of internet
culture, Agamben singles out the debasement of the face as one
of the ways in which language is disfigured and emptied of its
social efficacy. In an essay that draws on the work of Buber's
collaborator, Franz Rosenzweig, Agamben declares: "The face is
the only location of community . . . the face's revelation is revelation of language itself."[28] Pointing to how the face is exploited
and debased in advertising, pornography, and many other
domains, he writes that the face is the object of "a global civil
war whose battlefield is social life in its entirety . . . whose
victims are all the peoples of the earth." Now, twenty-five years
since these reflections, there is no limit on the extent to which
the gaze, the voice, and the face can be split off from social
spaces and interpersonal association. They are made into objects
of monitoring and analysis for a variety of purposes and uses,
but the overriding goal is the smoother assimilation of humans
into machine systems and operations, a goal that requires the

narrowing and standardization of our reactions to people, events, and exchanges of many kinds.

Now there is an expanding use of voice analysis to identify the emotional mood of a speaker through auditory features of pitch, tone, speed, and volume, making it possible to quantify how "positive" or "negative" a speaker feels about a subject under discussion or about their interlocutors. As more platforms become voice-powered, human speech is processed into behavioral information, and robotic voices are made to simulate emotional interactions with users, while being continuously upgraded to seem more "likable" and "trustworthy." "Personal assistants" create feedback loops in which a machine can modify its performance based on determinations of mood or sentiment. In popular culture there have been many, mostly sanguine or comedic, characterizations of human–robot conversations, to the point of trivializing the phenomenon. We repeatedly are told that machines are becoming more human—an absurd, fatuous claim because it presupposes a neoliberal/corporatist notion of what "human" is.

Most of the innumerable shadings of how words can be articulated and sequenced become irrelevant in machinic transactions, despite the purportedly "lifelike" modeling of robotic speech. As machine voices become more pervasive, we lose the sensitivity to discriminate between lifeless, simulated sounds and the embodied vocalizations of a human being. The meaningful content of human speech is inseparable from its bodily performance: the rhythm of breathing, the movements of the folds and muscles of the larynx, the actions of mouth and tongue. For thousands of years, one of our primary means of understanding others has been our intuitive sensitivity to what is conveyed by these resonances and vibrations of a living voice. Now when talking to robots, we involuntarily flatten and diminish the breadth of expressiveness in our own words, and there is a withering of singularity and spontaneity in many of our other verbal interactions. An utterance is now often the equivalent of flicking an on/off switch. So what, some will reply: hasn't language always been a praxis, a way of doing things? This retort is either naïve or cynical, because it ignores the powerful institutional and financial circuitry within which spoken words are now solicited and deployed by data-driven procedures.

The expropriation and depletion of speech, of course, is not new. The radio and television era certainly accustomed everyone to the sound of lies uttered by voices emptied of human purposiveness, but this is now occurring on an immense and programmatic scale. The late Icelandic composer Jóhann Jóhannsson crafted a work in 2016 with recordings of short-wave radio broadcasts from the Cold War. These were from the so-called Numbers Stations on which intelligence agencies in the 1960s and '70s transmitted coded messages. In this piece, "Song for Europa," we hear the mechanical, flattened voice of a young girl repeating seemingly random sequences of numbers. Over her bleak recitation, Johansson sets an elegiac ascending harmonic pattern played by a string ensemble, highlighting not just the capture and depersonalization of the child's voice but the larger ways in which modern forms of power injure the most precious and vulnerable elements of human connectedness.

The prevalence of such inanimate and repetitive exchanges further disables one's aptitude or patience for the frustrations and inconclusiveness of meeting, speaking, and being with others. For the past fifteen years, much of the world has become habituated to monetized forms of communicating that isolate a speaker or sender in controllable, one-way circuits. At the same time, the internet has fostered a culture of prying and exposure: everything deemed worth knowing about someone is quickly searchable and retrievable. Whatever might be learned of another over time, through earned mutuality and unconcealedness, is of no material value or relevance. We are losing the possibility of listening; of facing, with forbearance, a stranger, someone destitute, someone who offers nothing to our self-interest. We are even less able to understand the difficulties of being present to someone, or to accept that dialogue may open up not on connectedness or fellowship but onto the unknowability of others. Corporate-designed forms of social media have eliminated the possibility of an ethical relation to otherness and affliction. In numerous ways, we are induced or compelled to follow the routines of digital work and leisure and to align ourselves with their mediocrity and mindlessness. Like Kafka's Land Surveyor, we convince ourselves that our goals and aspirations can be achieved through a dutiful and numbing conformity with the precepts and regulations of a system we know to be malign.[29] We acquiesce out of passivity or convenience, and over time we come to have thoughts and gestures that are no longer our own.

We live surrounded by what philosopher Adi Ophir calls "superfluous evils," those many forms of unbearable suffering that could be prevented but that persist by design or neglect.[30] Given the brutalities and injustices plaguing the earth today, to some it may seem of secondary importance to foreground the ethical consequences of these techniques for scanning the gaze, the face, and the voice. However, if we aren't attentive to how neoliberal imperatives are harming the intimate fabric which upholds the interhuman, we become less and less capable of sustaining or even initiating the larger-scale struggles against imperial war, economic terror, racism, sexual violence, and environmental disaster. With a weakened ability to respond to others, there is no abiding sense of mutual accountability and no motivation to abandon the meager compensations of one's digital insularity.

One of the most noted and now banalized phenomena of contemporary urban life is the atomized crowd of individuals all seemingly absorbed by the contents of their screens. These all-too-familiar scenes, in any place of assembly, amplify the implosion of public space and constitute a ritual demonstration of the refusal of community demanded by neoliberalism. They are a portent of the loss of the encounter, of a lifeworld based on the indispensability of "being with others." Yet we are told that this is merely an annoying and inconsequential side effect of the productive workings of our digital age, to which we will become accustomed, or that such behavior will moderate over time. This splintering of a social world is based on the obligatory acting out of busy-ness, of self-occupation. It's irrelevant what anyone is actually doing, whether looking, working, texting, shopping, surfing, listening, gaming, or whatever. The result is mass acquiescence to an immaterial architecture of separation, sustained by the simulation of self-serving activity and indifference to anything external to that performance. In such circumstances, there is a nihilistic willingness to let the world lapse. It is an insularity without the restorative benefits of actual solitude; it is the pseudo-privatization of public spaces but without privacy. Obviously, capitalism has spawned many configurations of social alienation and separateness, as thinkers from Georg Simmel and Émile Durkheim to Guy Debord and Richard Sennett have shown. But, even in the mid-twentieth-century era of "the lonely crowd," public space was still latently charged with the unexpected or unforeseen, with possibilities of chance occurrences, meetings, or conversations which are now increasingly closed off.

The psychopathology of today's cellularization of public space was anticipated by Eugène Minkowski's clinical research of the 1930s, in which he characterized pervasive forms of mental illness as "a loss of vital contact with reality."[31] More explicitly, he saw this condition as a loss of the capacity for sympathy, "which is the most natural and most human aspect of our lives." In the undamaged individual, he wrote, sympathy surrounds all our perceptions like "a living fringe" that allows our responses to life with others to be "supple, malleable and human." The vibrancy of that fringe, of that awareness, both sensory and ethical, of the world at the periphery of whatever we may be doing is jeopardized by daily immersion in self-interested and privatized pursuits. The dwindling of care and attentiveness to others amplifies the "one-way discourse" and "generalized autism" that shape most activity online.[32]

Clearly, the neutralization of sympathy and the loss of a sense of responsibility reflect the larger disintegration of the moral scaffolding of everyday life. Alongside all of the tools for face, voice, and emotion recognition, our own capacity for recognition of the human begins to fail. The philosopher Paolo Virno has examined some of the consequences of the singular fact that "the human animal is capable of not recognizing another human animal as being one of its own kind. The extreme cases, from cannibalism to the colonial and European genocides, powerfully attest to this permanent possibility."[33] For Virno, this non-recognition is the limit at which the possibility of society begins to break down. The omnipresence of collectively occupied spaces marked by indifference to the proximity of others is inseparable from the scorched earth disaster of the present. It becomes a negative attunement to a world that is no longer shared.

Public spaces, as Alberto Pérez-Gómez has argued, have historically been milieus in which an enveloping mood drew a group together, allowing action to be experienced as purposeful and enabling individuals to feel part of a larger whole.[34] However, the mood or the atmospherics of now-atomized social spaces is disquieting, palpably toxic, and even more corrosive than is superficially evident. Cumulatively, there is a dissipation of curiosity about otherness or about the wondrous plenitude of non-human life. Experience is reduced to what can be instantly searched online. The Marxist theorist Ernst Lohoff has explored the violent parameters of life in a market-driven reality that dispenses with society to become composed only of individuals competing to succeed and survive on their own, whatever the cost. "The lunacy from which none are spared—having to exist as a self-sufficient subject—translates itself into the crazy impulse to defend this unlivable way of existence by any means necessary, even with a weapon in hand."[35] The individual's subjugation to the market is thus marked by delusions of autonomy and yet grounded in actual powerlessness. The rationalization and full economization of social relations "creates a greenhouse in which their immanent opposite, irrationality, always already charged with violence, thrives."

It is remarkable that at a moment of unparalleled danger for the future of the planet, for the very survival of human and animal life, that so many people should voluntarily confine themselves in the desiccated digital closets devised by a handful of sociocidal corporations. Pathways to a different world will not be found by internet search engines. Rather, what is needed is exploration and creative receptivity to all the resources and practices developed over the long history of human societies for thousands of years. There are enormous reserves of knowledge and insight, from all eras, about techniques of subsistence and the fostering of community that need to be recovered and adapted for present needs, especially from cultures in the Global South and indigenous peoples. Realistic strategies of resistance also require the invention of new ways of living. There must be a radical rethinking of what our needs are, of rediscovering our desires beyond the flood of shallow cravings that are promoted so unremittingly. At present, the main way in which we communicate with others is through what we buy, through the petty symbolic capital we strive to acquire, prompted by envy or the need for esteem. It would be a mistake to underestimate the intractability of individual dependence on the social distinction derived from the branded resources of consumption, but there is also reassuring evidence, in times of crisis or emergency, that attachments to material possessions and social status can quickly dissipate. For those with children, it means abandoning the desperate expectations these now carry to compete with their peers for individual success, and, instead, providing them with anticipations of a livable future built and shared in common.

But these are only the most preliminary tasks, only a necessary preparation for more difficult challenges ahead. Each region or cross-border community will determine its own pathways, but, as many now clearly recognize, the most urgent projects will include the expansion of local food production and distribution, the making available of basic health care and paramedical services, the protection of clean water supplies, and the equitable remaking of existing housing stocks. Both visionary innovation and pragmatic ingenuity will be needed for the reorganization of city neighborhoods, for the reclaiming of derelict spaces, for finding new uses for existing tools and materials, and enlarging a barter economy. Also important will be reconceiving the bonds between humans and animals, salvaging what remains of biodiversity, and recovering the spirit of festival and arts defined by group participation.

Writing in the late 1950s, with a different array of antagonisms at stake, Jean-Paul Sartre made the claim that scarcity is the basis for all human history. "History is born," he wrote, "from an imbalance which disrupts all levels of society." The intrinsic violence of organized scarcity produces "the unbearable fact of broken reciprocity and of the systematic exploitation of man's humanity for the destruction of the human." At this moment, the mounting scarcity caused by scorched earth capitalism is imperiling the survival of billions of people and other forms of life on our planet. The extreme social disequilibrium, the murderous deprivations and the ravaging of habitats essential for life are the result of what Sartre called "the praxis of other human beings." But he insisted that the response to this violence can be "common action" by groups and communities that have managed to rebuild, even provisionally, the wounded underpinnings of human relations. Isolated individuals can make the discovery "that common action is the sole means of reaching the common objective."[36] Although global capitalism is run through with irreparable cracks and fissures, it is still held together by individuals clinging to their separateness, their privacy, their freedom from other selves, and their fear of anything communal. The internet complex continues to mass produce these solitary subjectivities, to deter cooperative forms of association, and to dissolve possibilities for reciprocity and collective responsibility. The threshold of a post-capitalist world is not far off, a few decades at most. But, unless there is an active prefiguration of new communities and formations capable of egalitarian self-governance, shared ownership, and caring for their weakest members, post-capitalism will be a new field of barbarism, regional despotisms, and worse, where scarcity will take on unimaginably savage forms. Sartre saw that emerging insurgencies had a unique capacity to break free of subservience to "anti-social apparatuses" and to transform passivity and isolation into new forms of solidarity. Revolutionary groups, in responding to a state of emergency, he said, could define their own temporality and determine "the speed with which the future comes to it."[37] Now, over half a century later, amid the burning and pillaging of our lifeworld, there is little time left to meet up with a future of new ways of living on earth and with each other.

Notes

1

1. Alain Badiou, *Ethics: An Essay on the Understanding of Evil*, trans. Peter Hallward, London: Verso, 2012, p. 121.
2. For an analysis of "the magnitude of our failure to perceive the political dimension of technology," see Alf Hornborg, "Technology as Fetish: Marx, Latour, and the Cultural Foundations of Capitalism," *Theory, Culture and Society*, vol. 31 (2014): 119–40.
3. Ivan Illich, *Tools for Conviviality*, New York: Harper and Row, 1973, pp. 20–1.
4. See Jean Robert, "Energy and the Mystery of Iniquity," in *The Challenges of Ivan Illich*, eds. Lee Hoinacki and Carl Mitcham, New York: SUNY Press, 2002, p. 186.
5. Karl Marx, *Grundrisse*, trans. Martin Nicolaus, New York: Vintage, 1973, p. 539. See also Antonio Negri, *Marx Beyond Marx*, trans. Harry Cleaver et al., New York: Autonomedia, 1992, pp. 120–1.
6. Elena Pulcini, *The Individual without Passions*, trans. Karen Whittle, Lanham, MD: Lexington Books, 2012, pp. 129–30.
7. Guy Debord, *Comments on the Society of the Spectacle*, trans. Malcolm Imrie, London: Verso, 1990, p. 15.

8. Jean-Paul de Gaudemar, "The Mobile Factory," *Zone* 1/2 (1986): 286. First published in J.-P. de Gaudemar (ed.), *Usines et ouvriers. Figures du nouvel ordre productif,* Paris: Maspero, 1980. Italics added.

9. See Harold Innis, *Empire and Communication,* Oxford: Clarendon, 1950.

10. Nancy Fraser, *The Old Is Dying and the New Cannot Be Born,* London: Verso, 2019, pp. 13–14.

11. Kate Aronoff, "Inside the Dream Defenders' Social Media Blackout," October 6, 2015, opendemocracy.net.

12. Gustav Landauer, *Revolution and Other Writings,* trans. Gabriel Kuhn, Oakland, CA: PM Press, 2010, p. 201.

13. Cited in Eugene Lunn, *Prophet of Community: The Romantic Socialism of Gustav Landauer,* Berkeley: University of California Press, 1973, p. 224.

14. Retort Collective, *Afflicted Powers: Capital and Spectacle in a New Age of War,* London: Verso, 2005.

15. See Pierre Belanger and Alexander Arroyo, *Ecologies of Power: Countermapping the Logistical Landscapes and Military Geographies of the U.S. Defense Department,* Cambridge, MA: MIT Press, 2016.

16. "Peoples' Global Action," in *We Are Everywhere: The Irresistible Rise of Global Anticapitalism,* London: Verso, 2003, p. 100.

17. Jean Baudrillard, *Carnival and Cannibal, or the Play of Global Antagonism,* trans. Chris Turner, London: Seagull, 2010, pp. 23–5.

18. Aimé Césaire, *Discourse on Colonialism,* trans. Joan Pinkham, New York: Monthly Review Press, 1972, pp. 42–3. Emphasis in original.

19. Bernard Stiegler, *The Decadence of Industrial Democracies,* trans. Daniel Ross and Suzanne Arnold, Cambridge: Polity, 2011, pp. 7–13.

20. Bernard Stiegler, *Symbolic Misery, Volume 1: The Hyperindustrial Epoch*, trans. Barnaby Norman, Cambridge: Polity, 2014, p. 10.

21. Enrique Dussel, *Beyond Philosophy: Ethics, History, Marxism, and Liberation Theology*, Lanham, MD: Rowman and Littlefield, 2003, pp. 68–9.

22. Franco Berardi, *Heroes: Mass Murder and Suicide*, London: Verso, 2015, p. 88.

23. Ludwig Binswanger, *Being-in-the-World*, trans. Jacob Needleman, New York: Basic Books, 1963, p. 259.

24. Gilles Deleuze and Félix Guattari, *Anti-Oedipus: Capitalism and Schizophrenia*, trans. Robert Hurley, Mark Seem, and Helen Lane, New York: Viking, 1977 p. 341.

25. Roberto Unger, *The Religion of the Future*, Cambridge, MA: Harvard University Press, 2014, p. 26.

26. Susan George, *The Lugano Report: On Preserving Capitalism in the Twenty-First Century*, London: Pluto Press, 1999, p. 56.

27. Lewis Mumford, *Technics and Civilization*, New York: Harcourt, Brace and World, 1962 p. 195.

28. Carolyn Merchant, *The Death of Nature*, New York: Harper and Row, 1980.

29. Philippe Descola, *Beyond Nature and Culture*, trans. Janet Lloyd, Chicago: University of Chicago Press, 2013, p. 72.

30. See the characterization of the lifeworld in Jean Cohen and Andrew Arato, *Civil Society and Political Theory*, Cambridge, MA: MIT Press, 1992, pp. 427–28.

31. See Silvia Federici, *Re-Enchanting the World: Feminism and the Politics of the Commons*, Oakland, CA: PM Press, 2019, pp. 188–97.

32. The many important texts of this period included Murray Bookchin, "Ecology and Revolutionary Thought" [1965], in *Post-Scarcity Anarchism*, Berkeley: Ramparts Press, 1971; Paul Shepard and Daniel McKinley (eds), *The Subversive Science: Essays Toward*

an Ecology of Man, Boston: Houghton Mifflin, 1969; Lynn White Jr., "The Historical Roots of Our Ecological Crisis," *Science*, vol. 155 (April 1967); Richard A. Falk, *This Endangered Planet*, New York: Random House, 1971; Barry Commoner, *The Closing Circle: Nature, Man and Technology*, New York: Knopf, 1971.

33. Guy Debord, *A Sick Planet* [1971], trans. Donald Nicholson-Smith, London: Seagull, 2009.

34. Fredric Jameson, *Postmodernism, or, the Cultural Logic of Late Capitalism*, Durham: Duke University Press, 1991, p. ix.

35. Jacques Derrida, *Specters of Marx*, trans. Peggy Kamuf, New York: Routledge, 1994, pp. 80–5.

36. John Ruskin, *Modern Painters*, vol. 5, New York: John Wiley, 1879, p. 297.

37. Rosa Luxemburg, *The Rosa Luxemburg Reader*, eds Peter Hudis and Kevin Anderson, New York: Monthly Review Press, 2004, p. 64.

38. Ibid., p. 103.

39. Karl Polanyi, *The Great Transformation* [1944], Boston: Beacon, 1967, p. 3.

40. Ibid., p. 133.

41. See Henry A. Giroux, *Against the Terror of Neoliberalism*, Boulder, CO: Paradigm, 2008, pp. 91–7.

42. Félix Guattari, *The Three Ecologies*, trans. Ian Pindar and Paul Sutton, London: Bloomsbury, 2000, p. 21.

43. Hannah Arendt, *Responsibility and Judgment*, New York: Schocken, 2003, p. 160.

44. Hans Jonas, *The Imperative of Responsibility*, Chicago: University of Chicago Press, 1984, p. 19.

45. Jürgen Habermas, *The Theory of Communicative Action: Lifeworld and System*, trans. Thomas McCarthy, Boston: Beacon, 1987, pp. 390–1.

46. Henri Lefebvre, *The Production of Space* [1974], trans. Donald Nicholson-Smith, Oxford: Blackwell, 1991, p. 287.

47. Andreas Malm, *Fossil Capital: The Rise of Steam Power and the Roots of Global Warming*, London: Verso, 2016, pp. 301–2.

48. Robert Pogue Harrison, *Forests: The Shadow of Civilization*, Chicago: University of Chicago Press, 1992, pp. 51–2.

49. Steven J. Heims, *John von Neumann and Norbert Wiener: From Mathematics to the Technologies of Life and Death*, Cambridge, MA: MIT Press, 1980, p. 247.

50. Paul Virilio, *Pure War*, trans. Mark Polizotti, New York: Semiotext(e), 1983, p. 54.

51. Simone Weil, *The Need for Roots*, trans. Arthur Wills, New York: Putnam, 1952, pp. 43–4.

2

1. Charles Lyell, *Principles of Geology* [1833], New York: Penguin, 1997.

2. John Bellamy Foster, Brett Clark, and Richard York, *The Ecological Rift: Capitalism's War on the Earth*, New York: Monthly Review Press, 2010, p. 37.

3. See, for example, Robert Kurz, *The Substance of Capital*, trans. Robin Halpin, London: Chronos, 2016; and Ernst Lohoff and Norbert Trenkle, *La Grande Dévalorisation*, trans. Paul Braun, Gérard Briche, and Vincent Roulet, Paris: Post-éditions, 2014.

4. Robert Kurz, *World Crisis: Robert Kurz's Annotated Interview*, ed. Charles Xavier, New Charleston, SC: Create Space Independent Publishing, 2017.

5. Wolfgang Streeck, *How Will Capitalism End?* London: Verso, 2016, p. 58.

6. David Graeber, "Reply to Žižek," *London Review of Books*, vol. 29, no. 22 (November 2007): 7.

7. Georges Sorel, *The Illusions of Progress* [1908], trans. John Stanley, Berkeley: University of California Press, 1969.

8. See François Hartog, *Regimes of Historicity: Presentism and Experiences of Time*, trans. Saskia Brown, New York: Columbia University Press, 2015.

9. Joseph Gabel, *False Consciousness: An Essay on Reification* [1962], trans. Margaret Thompson, New York: Harper, 1978, p. 151.

10. See, for example, Wells's conclusion to his *The Outline of History*, New York: Macmillan, 1920.

11. Svetlana Alexievich, *Secondhand Time: The Last of the Soviets*, trans. Bela Sheyevich, New York: Random House, 2017, pp. 135–6.

12. Günther Anders, *Hiroshima est partout*, trans. Denis Trierweiler et al., Paris: Seuil, 2008, pp. 56–5.

13. Tiqqun, *The Cybernetic Hypothesis* [2001], trans. Robert Hurley, Pasadena: Semiotext(e), 2020, pp. 52–3.

14. Luis Suarez-Villa, *Technocapitalism*, Philadelphia: Temple University Press, 2009.

15. Nicholas Davies, "What Is the Fourth Industrial Revolution?" World Economic Forum, January 19, 2016, weforum.org.

16. Federico Campagna, *Technic and Magic: The Reconstruction of Reality*, London: Bloomsbury, 2018, p. 42–3

17. Robert Smithson, *The Writings of Robert Smithson*, ed. Nancy Holt, New York: NYU Press, 1979, p. 111.

18. Jacques Camatte, *This World We Must Leave and Other Essays*, New York: Autonomedia, 1995, p. 97.

19. Jean-François Lyotard, *The Postmodern Explained*, trans. Barry Don et al., Minneapolis: University of Minnesota Press, 1992, p. 18.

20. Alfred North Whitehead, *Science in the Modern World*, New York: Macmillan, 1925, p. 96.

21. See, for example, Max Weber, "Science as a Vocation" [1917], in *The Vocation Lectures*, trans. Rodney Livingstone, Indianapolis: Hackett, 2004, pp. 1–31.

22. Jean-Pierre Dupuy, *The Mark of the Sacred*, trans. M. B. DeBevoise, Stanford: Stanford University Press, 2013, p. 46.

23. Melinda Cooper, *Life as Surplus: Biotechnology and Capitalism in the Neoliberal Era*, Seattle: University of Washington Press, 2008, p. 11.

24. Zygmunt Bauman, *Mortality, Immortality and Life Strategies*, Stanford: Stanford University Press, 1992, p. 134.

25. Theodor Adorno, "Education After Auschwitz," in *Critical Models: Interventions and Catchwords*, trans. Henry Pickford, New York: Columbia University Press, 1998, pp. 198–201.

26. Norman O. Brown, *Life Against Death*, Middletown, CT: Wesleyan University Press, 1959, p. 286.

27. Günther Anders, "On Promethean Shame," in Christopher Müller (ed.), *Prometheanism: Technology, Digital Culture and Human Obsolescence*, London: Rowman and Littlefield, 2016, p. 50.

28. Lewis Mumford, *The City in History*, New York: Harcourt Brace, 1961, p. 527.

29. Walter Benjamin, *The Writer of Modern Life: Essays on Charles Baudelaire*, trans. Harry Zohn, Howard Eiland, and Edmund Jephcott, Cambridge, MA: Harvard University Press, 2006, p. 86.

30. Anna Tsing et al. (eds), *Arts of Living on a Damaged Planet*, Minneapolis: University of Minnesota Press, 2017, p. 7.

31. See Malcolm J. Rohrbough, *Rush to Gold: The French and the California Gold Rush 1848–1854*, New Haven: Yale University Press, 2013.

32. Ernst Bloch, *The Principle of Hope*, trans. Neville Plaice, Cambridge, MA: MIT Press, 1986, p. 49.

33. See Jean Comaroff and John Comaroff, *Millennial Capitalism and the Culture of Neoliberalism*, Durham: Duke University Press, 2001, pp. 22–6.
34. Norbert Elias, *The Society of Individuals*, trans. Edmund Jephcott, Oxford: Blackwell, 1991, p. 201.

3

1. Herbert Marcuse, *Eros and Civilization*, New York: Random House, 1961, p. 220.
2. Herbert Marcuse, *One-Dimensional Man: Studies in the Ideology of Advanced Industrial Society*, Boston: Beacon Press, 1964, p. 158.
3. See Bernard Stiegler, *The Decadence of Industrial Democracies*, trans. Daniel Ross, Cambridge: Polity, 2011, pp. 62–3.
4. Edmund Husserl, *The Crisis of European Sciences and Transcendental Phenomenology*, trans. David Carr, Evanston, IL: Northwestern University Press, 1970, p. 46.
5. Ibid., p. 163.
6. Hannah Arendt, *On Revolution*, New York: Random House, 1963, pp. 232–3.
7. See Andreas Bernard, *The Triumph of Profiling: The Self in Digital Culture*, trans. Valentine Pakis, Cambridge: Polity Press, 2019.
8. See my *Suspensions of Perception: Attention, Spectacle, and Modern Culture*, Cambridge MA: MIT Press, 1999.
9. The Swedish company Tobii is a global leader in eye tracking technologies. See *tobiipro.com/fields-of-use/user-experience-interaction*. Emphasis added.
10. John Dewey, *Experience and Nature*, Chicago: Open Court, 1925, pp. 167–9.
11. From William Blake, "Vala or the Four Zoas," dated 1797.

12. Stan Brakhage, "On Filming Light" [1974], in *Stan Brakhage: Interviews*, ed. Suranjan Ganguly, Jackson: University Press of Mississippi, 2017, p. 56.

13. See Eric Hobsbawm, *The Age of Empire 1875–1914*, New York: Pantheon, 1987, pp. 243–62.

14. Alphonse Bertillon, "Tableau des nuances de l'iris humain," *Bulletin de la Société d'Anthropologie de Paris*, vol. 3, no. 1 (1892): 384–7.

15. Hanneke Grootenboer, *Treasuring the Gaze: Intimate Visions in Late Eighteenth-Century Eye Miniatures*, Chicago: University of Chicago Press, 2012.

16. Paul Shepard, *Man in the Landscape: A Historic View of the Esthetics of Nature*, College Station: Texas A & M University Press, 1967, p. 20.

17. Adolf Portmann, "The Seeing Eye," *Landscape: Magazine of Human Geography*, vol. 9, no. 1 (1959).

18. See Francisco Varela et al., *The Embodied Mind: Cognitive Experience and Human Experience*, Cambridge, MA: MIT Press, 1993, p. 163.

19. Georg Simmel, *On Individuality and Social Forms*, ed. Donald Levine, Chicago: University of Chicago Press, 1971, p. 330.

20. David Abram, *The Spell of the Sensuous: Perception and Language in a More-Than-Human World*, New York: Random House, 1997.

21. Boaventura de Sousa Santos, *The End of the Cognitive Empire*, Durham: Duke University Press, 2018, p. 93.

22. Jean-Jacques Courtine and Claudine Haroche, *Histoire du visage*, Paris: Rivages, 1988.

23. Avery Gordon, *Ghostly Matters: Haunting and the Sociological Imagination*, Minneapolis: University of Minnesota Press, 1997, pp. 4–5.

24. Sigrid Weigel, "Phantom Images: Face and Feeling in the Age of Brain Imaging," *Kritische Berichte*, vol. 40, no. 1 (January 2012).

25. Martin Buber, *I and Thou*, trans. Walter Kaufmann, New York: Simon & Schuster, 1970, p. 75.

26. Martin Buber, *The Knowledge of Man*, trans. Maurice Friedman, London: Allen and Unwin, 1965, p. 67.

27. Giorgio Agamben, *Means Without End: Notes on Politics*, trans. Vincenzo Binetti and Cesare Casarino, Minneapolis: University of Minnesota Press, 2000, p. 81.

28. Ibid., p. 90.

29. See Günther Anders, *Franz Kafka* [1951], trans. Anthony Thorlby, New York: Hillary House, 1960.

30. Adi Ophir, *The Order of Evils: Toward an Ontology of Morals*, trans. Rela Mazali and Havi Carel, New York: Zone Books, 2005, pp. 515–16.

31. Eugène Minkowski, *Lived Time: Phenomenological and Psycho-pathological Studies*, trans. and intro. Nancy Metzel, Evanston, IL: Northwestern University Press, 1979.

32. These two phrases are from Guy Debord, *The Society of the Spectacle*, trans. Donald Nicholson-Smith, New York: Zone Books, 1994, p. 153.

33. Paolo Virno, *Multitude: Between Innovation and Negation*, trans. Isabella Bertoletti, Los Angeles: Semiotext(e), 2008, pp. 181–2.

34. Alberto Pérez-Gómez, *Attunement: Architectural Meaning After the Crisis of Modern Science*, Cambridge, MA: MIT Press, 2016, pp. 28–30.

35. Ernst Lohoff, "Violence as the Order of Things" [2003], *Mediations*, vol. 27 (Fall/Spring 2013–14).

36. Jean-Paul Sartre, *Critique of Dialectical Reason* [1960], vol. 1, trans. Alan Sheridan-Smith, London: Verso, 2004, p. 387.

37. Ibid., p. 390.